Chinese Festivals

One of the most distinctive features of Chinese culture is the great variety of unique festivals that has evolved over the course of China's long history. Chinese festivals are deeply rooted in popular tradition, and despite China's many changes they remain firmly established as part of the country's vibrant culture. *Chinese Festivals* introduces a representative selection of these celebrated traditions with full-color illustrations, providing a flavor of the diversity of modern and traditional Chinese culture.

Introductions to Chinese Culture

The thirty volumes in the Introductions to Chinese Culture series provide accessible overviews of particular aspects of Chinese culture written by a noted expert in the field concerned. The topics covered range from architecture to archaeology, from mythology and music to martial arts. Each volume is lavishly illustrated in full color and will appeal to students requiring an introductory survey of the subject, as well as to more general readers.

Wei Liming

Chinese Festivals

CAMBRIDGE
UNIVERSITY PRESS

University Printing House, Cambridge CB2 8BS, United Kingdom

One Liberty Plaza, 20th Floor, New York, NY 10006, USA

477 Williamstown Road, Port Melbourne, VIC 3207, Australia

314-321, 3rd Floor, Plot 3, Splendor Forum, Jasola District Centre, New Delhi - 110025, India

79 Anson Road, #06-04/06, Singapore 079906

Cambridge University Press is part of the University of Cambridge.

It furthers the University's mission by disseminating knowledge in the pursuit of education, learning and research at the highest international levels of excellence.

www.cambridge.org
Information on this title: www.cambridge.org/9780521186599

Originally published by China Intercontinental Press as
Chinese Festivals (9787508516936) in 2010

This updated edition is published by Cambridge University Press
with the permission of China Intercontinental Press under
the China Book International programme.

For more information on the China Book International programme, please visit
http://www.cbi.gov.cn/wisework/content/10005.html

First published 2011

A catalogue record for this publication is available from the British Library

ISBN 978-0-521-18659-9 Paperback

Contents

Introduction

Chinese culture has a history of some five thousand years. During this time, a great variety of unique, traditional festivals has evolved. Chinese festivals are rooted deeply in popular tradition, and despite China's many changes they remain firmly established as part of its colorful culture.

Over time, increasing productivity, improved standards of living and the establishment and growth of religion have all contributed to the emergence and development of festivals.

Most of the festivals in ancient China were connected with the development of astronomy, the calendar and mathematics. Many developed from what became twenty-four seasonal division points under the traditional Chinese lunar calendar, all of which had been more or less established by the time of the Han Dynasty (206 BC–AD 220). People developed different customs in their work and daily lives to express their hopes and fears in connection with the yearly change of seasons and natural

"Joyful Peasants." Many different festivals and customs have been formed on the basis of traditional agriculture.

Twenty-Four Seasonal Division Points					
Season	Division Points	Solar calendar	Lunar calendar	Ecliptic (degree)	Significance
Spring	Beginning of Spring	4–5 Feb.	Early first lunar month	315	Spring begins
	Rain Water	19–20 Feb.	Middle first lunar month	330	The amount of rain increases
	Waking of Insects	4–5 Mar.	Early second lunar month	345	Hibernating animals are woken by the spring thunder
	Vernal Equinox	20–21 Mar.	Middle second lunar month	0	The sun shines above the Equator and the day and night are of equal length
	Pure Brightness	5–6 Apr.	Early third lunar month	15	Pure and bright; trees and grass flourishing
	Grain Rain	20–21 Apr.	Middle third lunar month	30	The rainfall begins to increase and crops grow well
Summer	Beginning of Summer	5–6 May	Early fourth lunar month	45	Summer begins
	Grain Budding	21–22 May	Middle fourth lunar month	60	Grains begin to form
	Grain in Ear	6–7 Jun.	Early fifth lunar month	75	Crops such as wheat begin to ripen
	Summer Solstice	21–22 Jun.	Middle fifth lunar month	90	The sun shines above the Tropic of Cancer and the day is at its longest
	Slight Heat	7–8 Jul.	Early sixth lunar month	105	Hot
	Great Heat	23–24 Jul.	Middle sixth lunar month	120	The hottest time
Autumn	Beginning of Autumn	7–8 Aug.	Early seventh lunar month	135	Autumn begins
	Limit of Heat	23–24 Aug.	Middle seventh lunar month	150	The summer heat begins to cool
	White Dew	7–8 Sep.	Early eighth lunar month	165	Colder and morning dew begins to appear
	Autumnal Equinox	23–24 Sep.	Middle eighth lunar month	180	The sun shines above the Equator and the day and night are equal
	Cold Dew	8–9 Oct.	Early ninth lunar month	195	Getting colder and the morning dew is very cool
	Frost begins	23–24 Oct.	Middle ninth lunar month	210	Getting colder and frost begins to appear

Season	Division Points	Solar calendar	Lunar calendar	Ecliptic (degree)	Significance
Winter	Beginning of Winter	7–8 Nov.	Early tenth lunar month	225	Winter begins
	Slight Snow	22–23 Nov.	Middle tenth lunar month	240	Light snowfall
	Heavy Snow	7–8 Dec.	Early eleventh lunar month	255	Heavy snowfall
	Winter Solstice	22–23 Dec.	Middle eleventh lunar month	270	The sun shines above the Tropic of Capricorn and the day is at its shortest
	Slight Cold	5–6 Jan.	Early twelfth lunar month	285	Cold
	Severe cold	20–21 Jan.	Middle twelfth lunar month	300	Extremely cold

phenomena. Based on these customs and activities, Chinese festivals began to take shape.

It is thought that many Chinese festivals originated in the pre-Qin Dynasty (before 221 BC), such as New Year's Eve, New Year's Day, Lantern Festival, *Shangsi* Festival, *Hanshi* Festival, Dragon Boat Festival, Double Seventh Festival and Double Ninth Festival, but they developed and spread over the centuries. The original customs were related to primitive worship and superstitions and often involved colorful legends and stories. Religion was another influence, as were certain historical figures.

Yangjiabu New Year prints, late Qing Dynasty.

By the time of the Han Dynasty, the major traditional Chinese festivals had been established. The Han Dynasty was the first golden period after the unification of China when the nation enjoyed political and economic stability, and science and

technology were developing rapidly. Regional cultures such as the Qin, Chu and Qi-Lu, which had had a long history, integrated over time and emerged as the cultural community of the Han. All these factors favored the establishment of festivals.

The Tang Dynasty (618–907) saw festivals evolving from primitive sacrifices and superstitions and becoming increasingly like a kind of entertainment. Festivals became more joyful events. Increased communication between different nationalities and the development of religion added new vigor to the culture of festivals, and ensured that they would last to the present day.

Traditional Chinese festivals are not only an important part of the cultural life of the Chinese people; they also play a special role in trade and communication. Almost every festival is an opportunity for trading and socializing. In these festivals, farmers exchange produce, townspeople buy goods, scholars share their work and the government stages grand events to establish or reaffirm moral principles.

The development of festivals happens over a long period, and the nature of traditional Chinese festivals reflects the rich and vibrant history of the Chinese nation. The Han people have some important festivals, but the other fifty-five ethnic groups of China also have their own particular festivals and customs. Their ancient origins and customs, which have lasted to the present day, give an indication of how others lived in the past. Observing or even participating in these colorful festivals can give a sense of the essence of Chinese culture.

Society has developed, attitudes have changed, and the culture of Chinese festivals evolves continuously. Since the Revolution of 1911, China has seen different styles of festivals co-existing with each other. Some have flourished and others have dwindled. On the one hand, a few important festivals,

A couple celebrating their golden wedding anniversary present each other with roses for Valentine's Day.

including the Spring Festival, Pure Brightness Festival, Dragon Boat Festival and Mid-Autumn Festival, are still widely celebrated. They have inherited the essence of the traditional festivals, but have also developed and adopted some new features. Some less important festivals, on the other hand, were gradually forgotten over the years. Recently, some western festivals have been introduced into China, and these "foreign festivals" such as Valentine's Day, April Fool's Day, Mother's Day and Christmas Day are becoming increasingly popular among Chinese people, especially among younger generations living in urban areas.

As people's living conditions improve and their lifestyles change, ways of celebrating festivals change. Tradition and innovation combine and many people have abandoned traditional customs, celebrating the festivals in a more simple and casual way. For example, the internet and mobile phones have brought a new way for people to exchange good wishes.

Chinese festivals and the way Chinese people enjoy them are becoming more diverse and exciting.

The festivals introduced in this book represent only a small number of the many and varied Chinese festivals, but it is hoped they will give a flavor of the charm of traditional Chinese culture.

A beautifully decorated Christmas tree.

Traditional Festivals

China covers a large area and has a number of ethnic groups. The various regions and ethnic groups have different customs concerning food, clothing, housing and transport, festivals and religion, all of which have lasted for hundreds of years and have become part of their culture. Some customs, however, are shared by all Chinese people and have merged into mainstream Chinese culture.

Laba Festival

Name: *Laba* Festival
Date: the eighth day of the twelfth lunar month

In China, the twelfth month of the lunar year is called "*la* month," and the eighth day of the twelfth lunar month is called "*Laba* Festival" (*ba* means "eight" in Chinese) or "*la* day." *Laba* Festival is a tradition of the Han people. It is also regarded as the prelude to the Spring Festival.

The *Laba* Festival is thought to have originated from the ancient Chinese *la* ceremony. Agriculture has always been very important in China. Whenever there was a good harvest, the ancient people would consider it to be the blessing of the gods and would hold a grand ceremony to celebrate it, called a "*la* ceremony." After

Two "Old Beijingers" enjoying *laba* porridge.

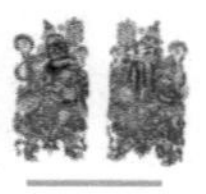

the ceremony people would entertain their fellow villagers with the porridge they had made from their newly harvested broomcorn millet. Everybody would gather together to enjoy the celebrations. The *la* ceremony later developed into a festival mainly to commemorate ancestors. In the fifth century, the government set the eighth day of the twelfth lunar month as the *Laba* Festival.

After the spread of Buddhism into China, people developed another story based on the traditional custom of honoring the ancestors and eating porridge, saying that the eighth day of the twelfth lunar month was the day when Sakyamuni, the founder of Buddhism, became a Buddha. The story goes that Sakyamuni had practiced Buddhism for many years and through his fasting he had become so thin that he resembled a bag of bones. He was about to abandon his fast when a shepherd girl gave him rice and porridge, which restored his strength and brought him back to the right train of thought. Contemplating under the Bodhi tree, he finally became a Buddha on the eighth day of the twelfth lunar month. To commemorate this event, on this day every year Buddhists began to make porridge with rice and dried fruits to make offerings to the Buddha, and the porridge was called "*laba* porridge."

The Chinese have been eating *laba* porridge since the time of the Song Dynasty (960–1279). In those days, the central and local government as well as the monasteries would make *laba* porridge on every *Laba* Festival. This custom became particularly popular during the Qing Dynasty (1644–1911). The emperor, empress and princes would give *laba* porridge to their officials and servants and send rice and fruit to the monasteries. In addition, every family would make *laba* porridge to honor their ancestors. People got together to enjoy the food with their family members and shared it with other families to show their good wishes.

There are many kinds of *laba* porridge. The traditional *laba* porridge should include eight main ingredients and eight extra ones, in accordance with the "*ba*" in "*laba* porridge" which suggests good luck ("*ba*," in Chinese, is usually related to "*fa*," which means prosperity). The main ingredients are usually beans such as red beans, mung beans, cowpeas, haricots, peas and broad beans and grains such as rice, millet, polished round-grained rice, sticky rice, wheat, oat, corn and broomcorn millet. The additional ingredients usually include preserved peaches, preserved apricots, walnuts, jujube paste, chestnuts, persimmons, melon seeds, lotus seeds, peanuts, hazelnuts, pine nuts, preserved pears and raisins.

The main ingredients are put into a pot of water and cooked on a low heat. When this has been done, sweet flavourings such as sugar, rosewater and sweet osmanthus will be added. *Laba* porridge varies in different areas in China, the most delicate one coming from Beijing. In this variant there are more than twenty additions to the rice, such as jujube, lotus seeds, nuts, chestnuts, almonds, pine nut kernels, longans, hazelnuts, raisins, water chestnuts, roses, red beans and peanuts.

People usually start to prepare the porridge on the night of the seventh day of the twelfth month. They wash the rice, soak the fruit in water, pick out the best fruits, peel them, remove the stones and finally begin to cook them from midnight. It will be kept on a low heat until the next morning when the *laba* porridge is finally ready.

If the family takes the festival seriously, they will pay special attention to the color of the porridge. Dark-colored beans will not be used. Only polished glutinous rice, "seeds of Job's tears," water chestnuts and lotus seeds are chosen as ingredients and made into porridge. The white porridge served in exquisite bowls is not only delicious but also an attractive sight. Moreover, it is

Pickling *laba* garlic.

also a sign of good luck and a bumper harvest. The Chinese enjoy having the whole family around the table eating delicious *laba* porridge. Some people carve the fruits into shapes of people or animals or, after coloring the food with jujube paste, bean paste, tomatoes or haw jelly cakes, will knead them into the shapes of legendary figures.

When the *laba* porridge is done, it should first be offered to gods and ancestors as a sacrifice. Next will be relatives and friends living nearby, and the porridge must be sent out by noon. Finally the whole family will enjoy it together. Leftover *laba* porridge, even after several days, is considered a good omen since it suggests that there will be leftovers every year. What is more, if you share the porridge with the needy, it will be seen as a sign of virtue.

Besides cooking *laba* porridge, people in northern China also make "*laba* garlic" on *Laba* Festival. People peel the garlic, put it in jars and fill the jars with vinegar. Then these jars are sealed on the *Laba* Festival and placed in a warm room. When it comes to New Year's Eve and the family is ready to eat *jiaozi* dumplings, the garlic will be brought to the table. The pickled garlic cloves take on a jade-green color, contrasting attractively with the red vinegar.

Preliminary Year

Name: Preliminary Year (*Xiao Nian*)
Date: the twenty-third day of the last lunar month

The twenty-third of the last lunar month, or "preliminary year," is a day when people offer sacrifices to the Kitchen God.

The "monarch of the kitchen" or "Kitchen God," who is traditionally worshipped by the Chinese, is a god who controls

"Kitchen God," New Year poster.

"Door Gods," New Year poster from Yangliuqing, Tianjin, Qing Dynasty.

Yuhuang Dadi

Also called the "Jade Emperor," Yuhuang Dadi is the most powerful and high-ranking god in Taoist belief. The Jade Emperor is depicted as the governor of Three Worlds (upper, middle, lower), Ten Directions (Four Directions: east, south, west, north; Four Dimensions: northeast, northwest, southeast, southwest; Up and Down), Four Modes of Reproduction, and the fortunes of Six Realms (known as Deva, Manusya, Asura, Naraka, Tirzane, Preta). People worship the Jade Emperor as the king of the gods. In Taoism the Ninth Day of the First Month in the lunar calendar every year is taken as the birthday of the Jade Emperor.

the fortune of families. It is said that on the twenty-third day of the twelfth lunar month every year, the Kitchen God will report to Yuhuang Dadi (the Jade Emperor, the supreme deity in Taoism) about the good and evil deeds of each family over the past year so that Yuhuang Dadi can decide whether they should be rewarded or punished. When it is time to send the Kitchen God on his way, people will put candies, water, soybeans and fodder in front of his statue or paper effigy. The last three are prepared for the horse on which the Kitchen God goes to heaven. When giving offerings to him, people will melt *Guandong* candy (originating in Northeast China) and

apply it to the Kitchen God's mouth. With his mouth glued, he will not be able to speak ill of others to Yuhuang Dadi. Chinese people follow the custom that "men do not worship the moon and women do not revere the kitchen," therefore the ceremony of offering sacrifices to the Kitchen God is only performed by men.

On New Year's Eve, the Kitchen God will come to earth with other gods to celebrate the Spring Festival, so there is a ceremony for "welcoming the Kitchen God."

People always begin to clean their houses on the eighth day of the twelfth lunar month and this usually lasts until the twenty-third day. The house is thoroughly cleaned, with the aim of banishing bad luck and giving it a fresh appearance. The twenty-fourth day of the last lunar month is designated as "house cleaning day" in Beijing. Every year when it comes to that day, housewives will cover the beds and furniture and also their heads, and then they will brush the walls with brooms and clean the tables and floors.

Spring Festival

Name: Spring Festival (*Chun Jie*)
Date: the first day of the first lunar month

Every year the end of winter and the coming of spring heralds the first traditional festival of the year. The Spring Festival (New Year of the lunar calendar) is a major celebration for the Chinese. It is the grandest and most exciting festival, with a long history and rich cultural connotations.

Lion dancing during the Spring Festival.

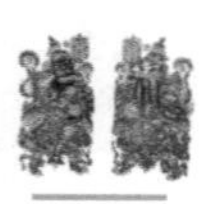

"Celebrating the New Year," New Year poster. Courtesy of Li Lulu.

Spring Festival is at the beginning of the lunar year, commonly called *Guo Nian*. Over the course of two thousand years, Chinese New Year customs have emerged, developed and changed. These customs started to appear in the Pre-Qin period. At that time, people held celebrations after the farming year was over as a sacrificial activity to acknowledge the gods' beneficence. "July," in *The Book of Songs*, records festive customs over two years in the Western Zhou period (1046–771 BC), when people offered wine and lamb to the gods as thanks for their blessings during the past year and as an invocation for favorable weather and a good harvest in the coming year. There was no fixed date for these celebrations because different states used different calendars, but it generally fell around the time in winter when agriculture was quieter, and was the fore-runner of New Year customs in later generations.

New Year customs were formalized during the Han Dynasty. After the social tumult at the end of the Warring States Period (475–221 BC) and the Qin Dynasty, the government of Western Han (206 BC–AD 25) attempted to restore social order. People were more optimistic and a series of festive customs resulted. The adoption of the *Taichu* Calendar stabilized the calendar system and the first day of the first lunar month was set as the first day of the year. As a result, the worship of gods, sacrifices and celebrations that had been held previously at various times in late winter or early spring were gradually brought together on the first day of the first lunar month. By the time of the Southern and Northern dynasties (420–589) people would set off fireworks, exchange Spring Festival couplets, drank *tusu* wine, stay up all night on New Year's Eve, light lanterns and so on. The Spring Festival was becoming the most important festival in China.

Taichu Calendar
The calendar brought into operation in the Han Dynasty. Emperor Wu of Western Han, on the advice of Sima Qian (born around 140 BC) and others, ordered Luoxia Hong, Deng Ping and other astronomers to formulate this calendar. The "Taichu Calendar," a relatively comprehensive calendar in Chinese history, set the first month of spring as the beginning of a year, incorporated the twenty-four seasonal divisions, and recorded the cycle of solar and lunar eclipses.

New Year customs changed in the Tang Dynasty (618–907). This was a time of economic prosperity and political progress as well as frequent contact between Chinese and foreign cultures. New Year customs gradually lost the mystic atmosphere of invocation and superstition, becoming entertaining and ceremonial celebrations. Fire crackers at New Year, for example, were no longer a means of keeping away ghosts and preventing evil, but were simply for fun.

New Year customs changed again during the Ming (1368–1644) and Qing dynasties (1644–1911), in two significant ways. First, their ceremonial and social function increased. At New Year, high officials gave each other their cards or went to each other's houses and ordinary people presented gifts and paid each other New Year visits. Second, their recreational aspect developed. During the New Year period, there

were all kinds of activities – the lion dance, the dragon dance, drama, story-telling and stilt-walking. Beijingers visited the Changdian Temple Fair, Guangzhou people went to the flower market, Suzhou people heard the toll of the Hanshan Temple bell and Shanghai people went to the Town God's Temple. Activities varied from place to place, with new ones being introduced regularly. New Year customs absorbed Chinese culture, and became a way of celebrating traditions dating back thousands of years in one festival.

During the New Year period the Han people and most other nationalities in China hold various celebrations, which usually feature sacrifice to a deity or the Buddha, memorial sacrifices to ancestors, embracing joy and receiving good fortune, and expressing hope for a good year. These celebrations vary and have different national characteristics.

New Year has been a major celebration in China for more than two thousand years. It involves almost everyone and is

A New Year poster from the Qing Dynasty, "*Liannian Youyu* (Surplus Every Year)," expresses hopes for the coming year.

The red *fus* (good fortune) are often pasted on doors or windows for good luck.

deeply engrained in the lives of Chinese people all over the world. At the end of every lunar year, people who are away from home hurry back to be with their families. New-year customs such as staying up for the New Year, making *jiaozi* (Chinese dumplings), pasting up New Year couplets, making New Year visits and many other things have become part of the Chinese way of life. The Spring Festival customs of the Chinese have also spread to neighboring countries such as Vietnam, North Korea, South Korea and Japan, who also celebrate New Year in similar ways.

Spring Festival does not last for just one day, but includes many activities in the first lunar month. It finishes after the fifteenth day of the first lunar month, with the Lantern Festival. In fact, people start preparing for Spring Festival celebrations from as early as the twenty-third of the last lunar month of the previous year. During this time, families are busy with cleaning, shopping for the festival, sticking paper-cutouts on windows, putting up New Year posters, writing New Year couplets, cooking rice cakes and making all sorts of food, all in preparation for getting rid of the old and welcoming in the new. New Year's Eve is an important time for the family to get together. Family members sit around a table, enjoy a sumptuous New Year's dinner, and then sit together to chat or play games. Most of them stay up until the next morning, which is called *Shou Sui* in Chinese.

Shou Sui means not to sleep on the last night of a year and to stay up to welcome the New Year. There is an interesting story about the origin of this custom going back many generations. Many, many years ago, a strange, fierce beast called Nian (Chinese for year) lived deep in the mountains and thick forests. It looked – and was – ferocious, and ate everything from insects to humans. All would go pale on hearing its name. It was discovered that every 365 days Nian went to a human settlement to feed, usually appearing after sunset and going back to the mountain or forest when the cock crowed dawn.

Now that they knew when Nian was due, people were terrified on the night (which is called *Nian Guan* in Chinese) and they worked out different ways of surviving. When the night came, every family made dinner early, put out the fire and cleaned up, locked the door to all chicken pens and bullpens, sealed the front and back doors of the house, and had a New Year's dinner. Since people did not know what the future held after this dinner, it was extremely sumptuous. Before dinner they had to pay respects to ancestors for their blessing to help them get through the night and then every family member dined together around a table to show harmony and reunion. After dinner, no one dared sleep but all huddled together and chatted to gain courage. This became the custom of staying up on New Year's Eve.

This custom first developed in the Southern and Northern Dynasties (420–589). It featured in poems and articles in the Liang period (502–557). People lit candles or oil lamps to stay up all night, symbolizing that the light shone on all evil, plagues and diseases and drove them away, and anticipated good luck and fortune in the New Year. This custom has continued to the present day.

When the clock strikes twelve at midnight on New Year's Eve, people will eat *jiaozi* dumplings. In earlier times, midnight was called *Zi Shi*. People eat *jiaozi* at this time because it symbolises replacing the old and changing the year (which sounds similar to *jiaozi* in Chinese). Also, *jiaozi* are shaped like gold ingots, and putting plates of them on the table represents the hope of "making a big fortune in the New Year and keeping the gold ingots coming in," a custom which still continues.

Children particularly enjoy Spring Festival because they can receive money, called *Ya Sui Qian* money, on New Year's Eve. It is given to them by their elders with good wishes. It is presented in a red paper bag and is distributed to children

Eating dumplings for the New Year is a tradition in many Chinese families.

Staying up until dawn on New Year's Eve to welcome the new year.

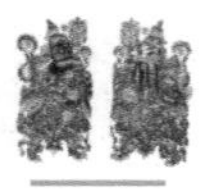

after the New Year's dinner or after the clock strikes midnight. It is said that since the word for year and the name of the evil spirit sound the same (both are *Sui* in Chinese), *Ya Sui* money can keep evil away from young people and ensure them a peaceful and healthy New Year.

From the first day of the lunar New Year people begin visiting relatives and friends and paying their New Year visits to each other. *Bai Nian* (Chinese for making a New Year visit) is an important Spring Festival custom and is a way of getting rid of the old, welcoming the new and expressing good will to each other. It is done out of respect for elders and love for relatives and friends. On these visits, people wish each other happiness, health, and all the best in the New Year.

During Spring Festival, people also have the custom of *Tie Chunlian* (pasting up New Year couplets). The original form of New Year couplets is the so-called *Tao Fu* (peach wood charm). These charms first appeared in the Zhou Dynasty (1046–256 BC) in the form of rectangular pieces of peach wood hung on each door. In ancient Chinese myth there is said to be a world of ghosts in which there is a mountain where a huge peach tree grows, covering an area of 3,000 *li*. On the treetop there is a golden rooster. Every morning when the golden rooster crows, ghosts that have wandered away at night will return to their world. The gate of this world is northeast of the peach tree with

The custom of pasting up rhymes continues to the present day. Photo by Chen Tingyou.

The annual CCTV New Year's Gala has become the focus of attention during the festival. Courtesy of Qin Xinmin.

gods standing at each side. If a ghost has done anything cruel in the night, these gods will discover it immediately and catch it, tie it up with ropes made of reeds, and send it to be eaten by tigers. Consequently all the ghosts in that world fear these two gods. People carve peach wood into their shapes and put them on their door to keep away evil and harm. Later, people simply carved the two god's names onto peach wood, believing this can also suppress evil. These carvings became known as "peach wood charms."

At the time of the Song Dynasty, people started writing couplets on peach wood. This had three purposes. First, it still had the function of the peach wood charm suppressing evil. Second, it expressed good wishes. Third, it was used as decoration. Later, couplets were written on red paper which symbolized happiness and fortune. They were stuck on doors and windows to show people's wish for luck in the coming year. New Year couplets have a history going back through the dynasties and have become a special form of folk art in China.

To wish for the whole family's fortune, long life, health and peace, people in some places still maintain the custom of pasting up a door god. It is said that with two door gods stuck on the door demons and ghosts will be scared away. The ancient Chinese believed that people with grotesque faces had magic power and superhuman ability. They were believed to be just and kind, and their role was to defeat ghosts and demons. Zhong Kui, a respected ghost-catcher in Chinese mythology, often painted on doors or gates, has a strange shape and an ugly face. This is why door gods always have angry, staring eyes and fierce expressions with various traditional weapons to hand, always ready to fight with ghosts that dare to challenge them. Since the door of a traditional Chinese house is in two parts, door gods usually appear in pairs. People often choose the figures of the door god Qin Shubao and Yuchi Jingde, two valiant generals who were chosen to protect Emperor Taizong of the Tang Dynasty when he was ill. Another popular choice is Shen Tu and Yu Lei, two ghost-catching gods.

"Baozhu Shenghua" (crackers bring flowers) by Wu Youru, late Qing Dynasty.

Setting off firecrackers is very popular with children during Spring Festival. Traditionally it was believed that crackers could drive away goblins and expel demons, so every year from New Year's Eve, the sound of crackers fills the air. The beautiful fireworks add to the excitement.

During Spring Festival, each region has its local traditional entertainments, with the lion dance, the dragon dance, the "land boat" dance and stilt-walking being the most common. Many regions hold temple fairs, which usually last from the first to the seventh of the first lunar month. Here there are wonderful performances of the lion dance and the dragon dance and various kinds of handicrafts and local delicacies on offer, attracting many thousands of people.

Spring Festival has changed over time. For example, many cities have forbidden or restricted fireworks and crackers on the grounds of fire risk or pollution. But this does not spoil the fun. On New Year's Eve, families still get together and have a New Year's dinner while watching the New Year's Gala on

Temple fair at Changdian in Beijing.

television until early in the morning of the first day of the first lunar month.

The official holiday at Spring Festival is three days, but in practice people usually have a seven-day holiday plus the two weekends before and after this major Chinese festival.

Yuanxiao Festival

Name: *Yuanxiao* Festival (Lantern Festival)
Date: the fifteenth day of the first lunar month

The fifteenth day of the first lunar month is the traditional Chinese *Yuanxiao* Festival. Because the first lunar month is also called "*yuan* month" the night of the fifteenth day of yuan month is the first full moon; *xiao* means "night," so the festival is named *Yuanxiao* Festival or *Shang Yuan* Festival, *Yuanxi* Festival or Lantern Festival.

"Celebrating the Lantern Festival," New Year poster, Qing Dynasty.

The Chinese people have a custom of enjoying lanterns on Lantern Festival. The custom comes from the Taoist "Theory of Three Yuan": the fifteenth day of the first lunar month is *Shang Yuan* Festival; that of the seventh lunar month is *Zhongyuan* Festival; and that of the tenth lunar month is *Xia Yuan* Festival. These three *yuan* denote heaven, earth and water, with three corresponding "officials." Because the "official of heaven" is happy and likes joyful, bright things, lanterns should be lit on *Shang Yuan* Festival. The custom of lighting lanterns on Lantern Festival had already appeared in the Han Dynasty. Through the generations, more and more varieties of lanterns have been created. For example, there are mirror-like lanterns, phoenix lanterns, colored-glaze lanterns and so on. Fireworks are also popular during this festival. "Shining trees and sparkling fireworks weave a sleepless night" goes a Chinese saying describing the night of Lantern Festival.

The game of solving lantern riddles is also traditionally played on the Lantern Festival. Lantern riddles are a game with Chinese characters. The answer to a riddle is hidden behind a beautiful poem or some common sayings written on the paper stuck to the festival lanterns. People try to solve them, rather like crossword clues. The game of solving lantern riddles first appeared in the Song Dynasty. In the capital Lin'an (now Hangzhou) of the Southern Song Dynasty (1127–1279), people would set and solve lantern riddles on Lantern Festival. Eating sticky rice balls is another characteristic custom of Lantern Festival, said to have originated in the Spring and Autumn Period (770–476 BC). The sticky rice ball is also called *tangyuan* or *yuanzi*, and is a small ball made of glutinous rice with or without stuffing (usually sugar, bean paste, hawthorn or other dried fruits). It can be boiled, fried or steamed. Eating sticky rice balls on the night when the moon is full for the first time in a year indicates people's wish for happy reunions and a peaceful life.

Captivated by lanterns at the Lantern Festival on the fifteenth of the first lunar month.

Over time, more and more activities were added to the Lantern Festival. In cities there are lantern ceremonies in which all kinds of lanterns are exhibited, and in the countryside there are activities such as setting off fireworks and walking on stilts. Other activities have appeared in some places such as playing with fabric lions, doing the *yangge* dance, playing on swings and playing *taiping* drums.

A father and son try to solve a lantern riddle amongst the crowd.

Spring Dragon Festival

Name: Spring Dragon Festival (the dragon lifts its head on the second day of the second lunar month)
Date: the second day of the second lunar month

According to folklore, the second day of the second lunar month is the time when the dragon in charge of the rain lifts its head. From that day on rainfall will increase gradually, so it is called the "Spring Dragon Festival" or "Dragon Head Festival." There is a common saying in the north of China that "the dragon lifts its head on the second day of the second lunar month and large barns will be full and small ones will overflow."

At the Spring Dragon Festival, families in most parts of northern China will go to wells or rivers to fetch water with their lanterns lit in the morning. Then they will come back home, burn incense and offer up sacrifices. This ceremony was called "attracting the dragon into the field" in ancient times. On this festival, every family should eat noodles, which means "lifting the dragon's head," fry cakes, which means "eating the dragon's gallbladder" (the Chinese believe that it is the gallbladder that determines one's courage) and pop corn so that "golden beans can blossom; the dragon god can return to heaven and send rain to the earth and crops can grow well."

There is a well-known story about the origin of the Spring Dragon Festival. In the Tang Dynasty, Wu Zetian came to power and became empress, which irritated Yuhuang Dadi in heaven. He ordered the four dragon gods who are in charge of the rain not to rain a single drop in three years. However, the dragon god in charge of the river of heaven could not bear to see people on earth being starved to death, so he broke Yuhuang Dadi's rule and secretly let it rain. Yuhuang Dadi became so angry that he imprisoned the dragon god under a mountain as a punishment, and a stele on the mountain read as follows:

The dragon king breaks the heavenly rules by dropping rain
And is subject to thousands of years of punishment on earth
If ever he wishes to go back to the heavenly palace
It will be only when golden beans give birth to flowers.

"The Dragon Lifts its Head on the Second Day of the Second Lunar Month," New Year Poster.

To save the kind-hearted dragon god, people looked everywhere for the golden beans. On the second day of the second lunar month the following year, people found the secret of golden beans when they were scattering the seeds of corn: since the corn is just like golden beans, could not one say that the golden beans blossom when the corn is popped? So every family began to pop corn and set up an altar to offer the blossomed "golden beans" as sacrifices. The dragon god lifted his head and saw all this. Knowing that people were trying to rescue him, he cried to Yuhuang Dadi, "The golden beans have blossomed, so please set me free!" Yuhuang Dadi had no choice but to call the dragon god back to heaven. From then on it became a custom to pop corn on the second day of the second lunar month.

It is usual in north China for monsoon rainfall to increase after the second day of the second lunar month, thus the festival also shows people's wishes for fine weather and a better harvest.

Pure Brightness Festival

Name: Pure Brightness Festival (Tomb-Sweeping Day)
Date: the seasonal division point Pure Brightness (April 4 or 5)

The Pure Brightness Festival remains very special among all the traditional Chinese festivals still popular today. It is a great festival as well as an important seasonal division point. Falling one hundred and seven days after the beginning of winter, and fifteen days after the Spring Solstice, around April 5, it plays a special part in the change of seasons. To understand the origins of the Pure Brightness Festival, we first need to learn about a festival which was once very popular—*Hanshi* Festival. *Hanshi* Festival fell one or two days before the

Sweeping a tomb on Pure Brightness Day.

Pure Brightness Festival, and was also called "Cold Festival" or "Smoke-Banning Festival." This day was celebrated to commemorate a loyal court official in the Spring and Autumn Period called Jie Zitui.

Jie Zitui was a capable minister in the state of Jin, whose prince was called Chong Er. Civil war broke out in Jin and Prince Chong Er had to escape abroad. During his difficult exile of about nineteen years, Jie Zitui had always been at the prince's side. He had even made broth out of the flesh of his leg to feed the prince when they were short of food. Later, when Chong Er became duke, known as Jin Wengong (Duke Wen of Jin), he handsomely rewarded those who had stood by him in his hardship, leaving out only Jie Zitui. Many people felt very indignant towards Chong Er on Jie Zitui's behalf and advised Jie to ask for a reward from the duke. But Jie despised people who looked for rewards and he packed his bags and retreated to Mian Mountain with his mother.

When Jin Wengong heard the news, he felt so ashamed that he took some people and went to the mountain to find Jie Zitui. However, the bumpiness of the mountain road and the thickness of the forest added great difficulty to the search. Someone suggested that they could set fire to the forest so that Jie would be forced out. Wengong took this advice and the fire raged all over the mountain. Nonetheless, Jie Zitui still did not appear. When the fire was out, people found that Jie had already died under a willow with his mother. What is more, a letter written in blood was found in a hole in the tree. It said:

Giving meat and heart to my lord,
Hoping my lord will always be upright.
An invisible ghost under a willow
Is better than a loyal minister beside my lord.
If my lord has a place in his heart for me,
Please reflect when remembering me.
I have a clear conscience in the nether world,
Being pure and bright in my offices year after year.

To commemorate Jie Zitui's death, Jin Wengong declared this day to be the *Hanshi* Festival and ordered that no fire should be permitted in the whole country on that day. The next year when Wengong went to hold a memorial ceremony on that mountain with other ministers, they found the willow had grown new shoots. So they named the willow "Pure Bright Willow" and christened the day after *Hanshi* Festival "Pure Brightness Festival."

As it is usually bright and clear on the Pure Brightness Day, people often go to sweep the tombs of their relatives, offer sacrifices to their ancestors, and go for a walk in the countryside and plant willows.

Traditionally, Chinese people have great respect for their elders, especially their ancestors. When the Pure Brightness Festival comes around, families will pay a solemn visit to the tombs of their forefathers. They weed the tombs, add new earth to them, burn incense and put some food and paper money there to show their sincere affection and respect for the dead. This is called *shangfen* or "sweeping the tombs." However, as cremation is gradually taking the place of burial, graves are becoming rarer. But people can commemorate their forefathers in other ways, or they can go to the martyrs' park and mourn for them by putting flowers and wreaths on the graves of fallen revolutionaries.

At the time of Pure Brightness Festival, the weather is becoming warmer; trees are in leaf and grass begins to grow; everywhere in the countryside is turning green – it is just the right time for people to into the outdoors and relax. They often go to the countryside with their friends for fresh air and blue skies, leafy trees, fresh grass and beautiful flowers. The ancient people called the custom of walking in the countryside *taqing,* so Pure Brightness Festival is also known as Taqing Festival. People wear a willow twig on their heads to keep away ghosts and disasters and pray for peace and happiness. There is also a custom of "picking shepherd's

During the Pure Brightness Festival students pay their respects to revolutionary martyrs.

"Flying Kites in the Spring Wind," New Year poster.

purse while walking in the countryside," which still continues today. Around the time of Pure Brightness Festival, girls and women will pick the herb and make dumplings with it. Some women also like to wear a shepherd's purse flower in their hair.

Flying kites, playing tug-of-war and playing on swings are also popular at Pure Brightness Festival. It is a perfect time to sow seeds, so there are many agricultural proverbs and activities connected with Pure Brightness Festival, as in the saying: "Plant melons and beans around Pure Brightness Festival." In ancient times people also planted willows on this festival, hence the ancient poem: "A street of willows covered with a green veil, weaves the Pure Brightness Day."

In China these is a one-day holiday for the Pure Brightness Festival.

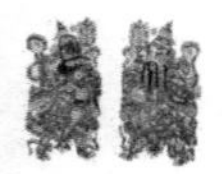

Dragon Boat Festival

Name: Dragon Boat Festival
Date: the fifth day of the fifth lunar month

There are many versions of the story of the origin of the Dragon Boat Festival, the most popular being that it is a festival commemorating Qu Yuan. This is the version that most Chinese people accept.

Qu Yuan (c. 340–278 BC) was a *dafu* (senior state official in feudal China) in the state of Chu during the Warring States Period. Among the seven states of that time (Qi, Chu, Yan, Han, Zhao, Wei and Qin), Qin was the most powerful and intended to conquer the other six and dominate the world. Qu's ability won the recognition of Chu Huaiwang (Huai King of Chu). However, Qu's opinion that Chu should carry out political reform and cooperate with the other states to fight against Qin met with opposition from his fellow officials. They spoke ill of Qu to Huaiwang. Huaiwang gradually became estranged from Qu, and in the end he drove Qu out of the capital of Chu. Finally, Chu was defeated by Qin. Grieving and indignant, Qu Yuan jumped into Miluo River and ended his life, on the fifth day of the fifth lunar month in 278 BC.

When people heard the news that Qu Yuan had drowned himself they were distraught, and rowed out to find his body but failed. To save the body from the fish, people threw food into the river to distract them. From that time on, people row dragon boats on rivers to mourn Qu Yuan on the fifth day of the fifth lunar month every year. They fill bamboo pouches with rice and throw them into rivers as a memorial ceremony. It was said that someone met Qu Yuan by the river and Qu said, "The food you gave me has been stolen by the dragon. You should wrap the rice in bamboo or reed leaves and fasten it with colored threads,

for these are things of which dragons are most afraid." Since that time, people began to commemorate Qu Yuan with *zongzi,* made of glutinous rice wrapped in bamboo or reed leaves, and thus *zongzi* has become the traditional food of the Dragon Boat Festival. The tradition of eating *zongzi* and rowing dragon boats has been handed down to later generations.

The second legend of the Dragon Boat Festival relates to a historical figure: Wu Zixu. Wu (d. 484 BC) was from the state of Chu in the Warring States Period. His father and brothers had been killed by the king of Chu and he sought refuge with the state of Wu and helped it fight all the way to the city of Ying, the capital of Chu. He exhumed the body of the king of Chu from the tomb and whipped it three hundred times in an act of revenge. Later the state of Wu became involved in a war with Yue. Wu Zixu advised the king of Wu not to compromise with Yue, but the king believed false stories about Wu Zixu and gave him a sword to commit suicide. Wu said, "After my death, please take out my eyes and hang them on the eastern door of the capital of Wu so that I can see Yue's army marching into Wu's land and conquering it." Then he killed himself. The King of Wu was annoyed by these words, and issued an order to put Wu Zixu's body in a leather bag and throw it into the river on the fifth day of the fifth lunar month. The Dragon Boat Festival is, therefore, also considered as a commemoration of Wu Zixu.

A third version of the origin of Dragon Boat Festival is said to honor Cao E, a loyal daughter in the Eastern Han Dynasty (25–220). Cao's father drowned in the river and the body could not be found for days. Cao E, who was only fourteen years old, cried day and night by the

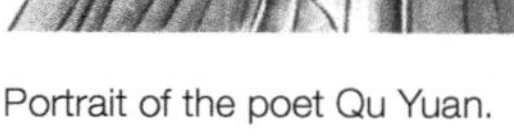
Portrait of the poet Qu Yuan.

Selling calamus.

river and finally jumped in on the fifth day of the fifth lunar month. Five days later, she returned with her father's body. To commemorate Cao E's loyalty, people built a "Cao E Temple" at the place where she jumped into the river. Her village was renamed "Cao E Village," and the river she jumped in became "Cao E River."

The Dragon Boat Festival has lasted for more than two thousand years in China. It is celebrated in more or less the same way in different areas, with Dragon-Boat races, eating *zongzi*, wearing perfumed sachets, and putting mugwort or calamus leaves around the home.

Dragon-Boat racing is a water sport which has had a long history in China, and is most common in the area south of the Yangtze River. In the twenty-ninth year of Qianlong's rule in the Qing Dynasty (1764), Taiwan began holding Dragon-Boat competitions, and Jiang Yuanjun, the magistrate of the Taiwan

Dragon-Boat racing in Hong Kong.

prefecture, presided over a friendly contest. Nowadays there are Dragon-Boat races in Taiwan and Hong Kong on the fifth day of the fifth lunar month every year. Dragon Boats have also found their way to countries such as Japan and Korea, and in 1980, the Dragon-Boat race was included in the list of the Chinese national sports events. The "Qu Yuan Cup" Dragon-Boat race is held every year. On June 16, 1991 (the fifth day of the fifth lunar month), the first international Dragon-Boat race Festival was held in Yueyang, the second city of Qu Yuan, Hunan Province. Before the competition there was a "Dragon-Head ceremony" which preserved the spirit of tradition and added some modern elements. The dragonhead was carried into the ancestral temple of Qu Yuan and was *shanghong* (draped with a length of red cloth) by a sportsman. Then the host delivered a funeral oration and *kaiguang* (drew the eyes) on the dragonhead. Then all the attendants bowed three times to the dragonhead, and it was finally carried to Miluo River—the competition site. Over 600,000 people attended the competition and festivities.

Reed leaves used to wrap *zongzi*.

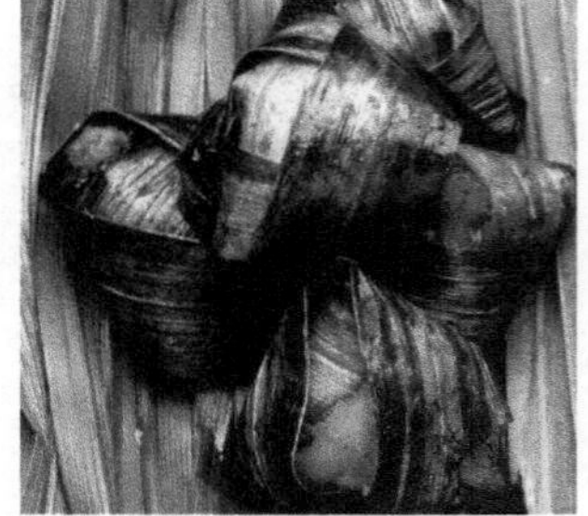

Zongzi (sticky rice cakes with meat stuffing).

Eating *zongzi* on Dragon Boat Festival is another important tradition among Chinese people. *Zongzi* has a long history and exists in many forms. It is recorded that early in the Spring-Autumn Period *zongzi* had appeared in an embryonic form as "horn millet," where the millet was wrapped in wild rice leaves, and "bamboo-wrapped *zong*," which was rice cooked in a sealed bamboo pouch.

During the Jin Dynasty (265–420), *zongzi* was accepted officially as the food eaten on Dragon Boat Festival. Then, in the Northern and Southern dynasties, mixed *zongzi*

appeared in which the rice was stuffed with meat, chestnuts, jujubes, red beans and such like. *Zongzi* could also be given to relatives and friends as presents. In the Tang Dynasty the rice used to make *zongzi* was "as white as the jade," and cone-shaped and diamond-shaped *zongzi* began to appear. The words *Datang zongzi* (*zongzi* in the Tang imperial period) even appeared in some Japanese literature. In the Song Dynasty *Mijian zong* (*zongzi* with glacé fruit) was popular. The poet Su Dongpo (1037–1101) also wrote about *zongzi* in his poem: "In *zongzi* I can always see waxberries." In the period of the Yuan (1206–1368) and Ming (1368-1644) dynasties, the leaves with which *zongzi* were wrapped changed from wild rice to bamboo leaves, and later reed leaves were also used. There were more varieties of added ingredients, such as bean paste, pork, pine nuts and walnuts.

To this day, Chinese families still soak glutinous rice, wash the bamboo or reed leaves and make *zongzi* when the fifth lunar month approaches. Jujube-stuffed *zongzi* are popular in the North, while stuffings such as bean paste, rice, ham and egg yolk are common in the South, where the *zongzi* of Zhejiang Province are the most typical. The custom of eating *zongzi* has been popular in China for thousands of years, even crossing the border and spreading to Korea, Japan and the countries of Southeast Asia.

"Zhong Kui," New Year poster.

A Chinese saying goes "wear willows on Pure Brightness Festival and use *aicao* (mugwort) on Dragon Boat Festival." People believe that the fifth lunar month is dangerous to health, as certain insects and germs come back to life to spread disease. So placing

mugwort and calamus around the home is regarded as an important activity on the Dragon Boat Festival. Every family will clean their doors and put the mugwort and calamus on the lintel or hang the plants from the ceilings to expel evil spirits and prevent diseases. *Aicao* is also called jia'ai or *aihao*. Its stalk and leaves contain a substance with an aroma which can drive away insects and keep the air crisp. The calamus is a perennial water plant. It has long narrow leaves that contain a substance which can refresh, strengthen bones and kill insects. This was the reason why the ancient Chinese people kept mugwort and calamus in their homes, and thus Dragon Boat Festival is also known as the "Health Festival."

Five poisonous creatures (snake, scorpion, toad, gecko and centipede).

Hanging Zhong Kui's picture to scare off ghosts is also a special custom during the Dragon Boat Festival. In the areas around the Yangtze River and the Huai River, people hang up a picture of Zhong Kui to guard their family from ghosts. The story of Zhong Kui goes like this: Emperor Xuanzong of Tang (r. 712–756) was suffering from a plague. One day he dreamed of two ghosts chasing each other in the imperial court. The younger ghost, wearing red, stole the scented sachet carried by Concubine Yang and the emperor's flute and ran around the imperial court. The elder one, wearing a gown and a cap, however, caught the younger one, dug out his eyes and swallowed them. Xuanzong cried out and the elder ghost said, "My name is

The White Snake
Originating in the Song Dynasty, this is one of the four major Chinese folk stories. In the story, a monster snake, Bai Suzhen (or Bai Niangzi), fell in love with Xu Xian and married him. However, her identity was discovered by a monk, Fa Hai, from the Jinshan Temple. On the advice of Fa Hai, Xu Xian persuaded Bai Niangzi to drink realgar liquor. Her original snake form was revealed, and Xu Xian was terrified to the point of death. Bai Niangzi stole immortal grasses from heaven to save Xu Xian, and fought against Fa Hai along with her maid, Xiao Qing (the Green Snake). She was defeated and imprisoned by Fai Hai underneath the Leifeng Pagoda. She was later rescued by her son. There are various popular operas on the theme of this story.

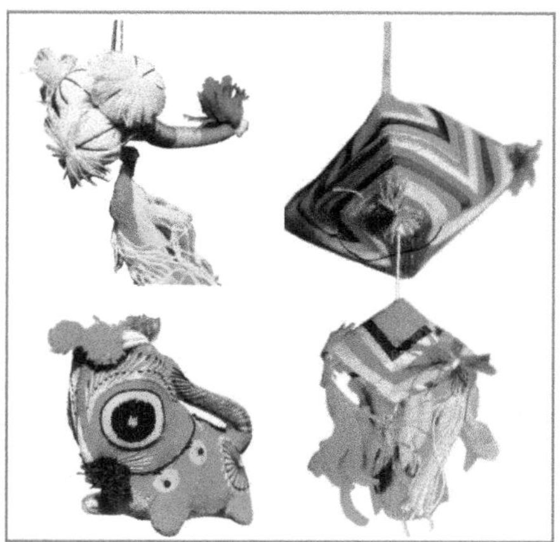

Various sachets.

Zhong Kui. I failed in the imperial examination, but I would like to help your majesty get rid of ghosts." When the king woke up, he was cured. Afterwards he asked Wu Daozi the painter to draw a picture of Zhong Kui based on his dream. Then he issued an order that the picture should be hung on the Dragon Boat Festival to guard against ghosts.

The custom of drinking realgar liquor is also very popular among people in the areas around the Yangtze River. There is a mineral containing sulfide in realgar liquor which can keep away snakes and insects. "The Story of a White Snake" which is still well-known today, includes a scene in which the human-shaped White Snake returns to her original form after drinking the realgar liquor. Thus people believed that poisonous creatures such as snakes, scorpions and centipedes could be scared off by realgar liquor, and drinking it could protect them from harm and keep them healthy.

There is also a custom of wearing perfumed sachets during the Dragon Boat Festival. The sachets are said to protect the wearer but are actually a kind of decoration on clothes. In the sachets there is usually vermilion, realgar and some aromatic substances. Wrapped in the silk, these fragrant materials give off a faint scent. Sachets come in all shapes, can be tied up with colorful threads and look very decorative.

The Dragon Boat Festival has developed into a very popular, grand festival in China, enriched by the ancient stories and legends behind it.

Double Seventh Festival

Name: Double Seventh Festival (the Praying-for-Cleverness Ceremony)
Date: the seventh day of the seventh lunar month

The seventh day of the seventh lunar month is the Double Seventh Festival in China. According to tradition, this is the day that Herd-boy and Weaving-girl are reunited. The beautiful love story behind the origin of this festival is still popular today.

It is said that long ago a clever and honest man named Niu Lang (Herd-boy) was living in the village of Niu west of Nanyang city. Niu Lang's parents died when he was very young and he had to live with his brother and sister-in-law. The latter was very cruel to Niu and always forced him to do hard work. Finally, she drove Niu out of her family. Poor Niu had only an old cow with him. One day the old cow said to Niu, "Tomorrow is the seventh day of the seventh lunar month; the seven daughters of Yuhuang Dadi will come to earth and bathe. The youngest one named Zhi Nü (Weaving-girl) is the cleverest. Hide her clothes and she will be your wife." Niu Lang was encouraged by what the cow had said and decided to give it a try.

"Herd-boy and Weaving-girl" by Wu Youru, late Qing Dynasty.

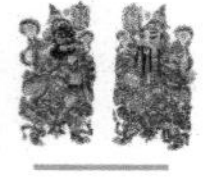

An American couple celebrates Valentine's Day, Chinese-style.

On that day, Niu Lang hid himself in the reeds by the river. Soon seven fairies descended from heaven. They took off their clothes and jumped into the river. At that moment Niu Lang jumped out of the reeds, grabbed Zhi Nü's clothes and dashed back. This terrified the seven fairies and six of them flew to heaven with their clothes on, leaving only the youngest, Zhi Nü, startled in the river. Niu Lang mumbled that he would return the clothes as long as she promised to marry him. Zhi Nü liked Niu Lang, so she nodded bashfully. After the marriage Herd-boy and Weaving-girl led a happy life and loved each other very much. Later they had a son and a daughter. However, the Queen Mother of the Western Heavens was irritated by their happiness and forced Zhi Nü to return to heaven.

Niu Lang then brought his children with him to heaven to bring Zhi Nü back. He had nearly reached her when the Queen Mother of the Western Heavens pulled a hairpin from her hair. With just one wave of the hairpin, she created a rushing river, which separated the two lovers, one on each bank. They could do nothing but weep together. Fortunately, all the magpies were moved by their sincere love. Hundreds of thousands of them flew there and they formed a magpie bridge so that Herd-boy and Weaving-girl could be reunited. This is said to be the origin of the Milky Way, with Herd-boy and Weaving-girl as the stars Altair and Vega. The Queen Mother of the Western Heavens could do nothing to stop this and she had to allow them to be reunited on the seventh day of every seventh lunar month.

Since then, on this day, young girls will dress in new clothes and try to find the Herd-boy and the Weaving-girl stars in the sky at night, expecting to see them reunited and praying to the gods that they can be as intelligent and talented as Zhi Nü and have a happy marriage. This is how the "Praying-for-Cleverness Ceremony" originated.

The Praying-for-Cleverness Ceremony is a very exciting day in the Chinese countryside. Young girls wear new clothes, worship the two stars and "pray to Zhi Nü for cleverness." There are many kinds of prayers, the most common one being for skill in threading needles. Young women bring out colorful threads and seven needles. The girl who can pull a thread through these needles will be regarded as a very talented lady.

The Double Seventh Festival is considered a kind of Chinese Valentine's Day. The story of Herd-boy and Weaving-girl reunited on the magpie bridge gives this festival a romantic flavor. It is said that you can even hear sweet whispers between the two lovers if you sit under a grape vine on the day of the festival.

"Threading the Needles" by Wu Youru, late Qing Dynasty.

Ullam-bana Festival

Name: Ullam-bana Festival (Ghosts' Festival or Zhongyuan Festival)
Date: the fifteenth day of the seventh lunar month

The fifteenth day of the seventh lunar month every year is "Ullam-bana Festival" or "*Zhongyuan* Festival," and in some places it is also called "Ghosts' Festival" or "*Shigu*." It is a Buddhist festival and also a day to offer sacrifices to the ancestors. Buddhists believe that hell is governed by Diguan Dadi. Every year on his birthday, which is the fifteenth day of the seventh lunar month, he will open the door of hell and all the ghosts will come to earth and people will be able to provide food and drink for them.

Ullam-bana comes from Sanskrit. It originated from a Buddhist ritual and means "to rescue those hanging upside down." It is said that a disciple of Sakyamuni saw his mother being hung upside down in hell and he asked the Buddha to release her soul from purgatory. Sakyamuni told him to prepare a hundred kinds of food for all the Buddhist monks in that area on the fifteenth day of the seventh lunar month so that his mother could be released. This was the beginning of "Ullam-bana Festival."

People began to follow this custom from the Liang Dynasty (502–557) in the Southern and Northern Period and it gradually became the *Zhongyuan* Festival. Later, in addition to providing food for the monks, activities such as *baichan* and *fang yankou* were added to the customs. On the day of the festival, the seat of the *fashi* (the person performing the ritual, usually a Buddhist) and the *shigu* platform will be prepared beforehand at the gate of the village. In front of the seat of the *fashi* is the Ksitigarbha Bodhisattva whose job is to release the souls of the ghosts in hell from purgatory, and dishes of flour, peaches and rice are laid on the ground. There are three memorial tablets and a flag on the *shigu* platform. When it comes to the afternoon, every family will place roast pork, lamb, chicken and duck and all kinds of cakes and fruits onto the *shigu* platform. The leader will stick a triangular paper flag of different colors into each offering, and the paper may read "grand ritual of Ullam-bana" or "the door of hell is open." The ceremony starts with a piece of grand, solemn religious music. Then the *fashi* takes the lead to strike the *muyu* (a wooden instrument hit by monks when chanting sutras) and chant an incantation. After this, flour, peaches and rice are scattered in all directions three times. This ceremony is called *fang yankou*.

When the night falls, every family will burn as much incense as they can to the Buddha on the ground in front of the door, which indicates that the crops will grow well.

Floating river lanterns are also popular on *Zhongyuan* Festival. A river lantern, or water lantern, is a lantern fixed on a small board. They are usually made of colorful paper and are usually shaped as lotuses. These lanterns will be lit and floated on the river. "Floating river lanterns" first started in monasteries and then became popular amongst lay people. According to tradition, river lanterns are floated to guide the spirit of those who died unjustly. When the lantern goes out, the task of guiding the spirit across *Naihe* Bridge (the bridge which dead people should cross in Buddhist legend) is complete. People believe that *Zhongyuan* Festival is a festival of ghosts, so it is also necessary to light lanterns and celebrate for them. But since ghosts are different from people, the lanterns in *Zhongyuan* Festival should also be different from those in *Shangyuan* Festival (Lantern Festival). As a result, lanterns in *Shangyuan*

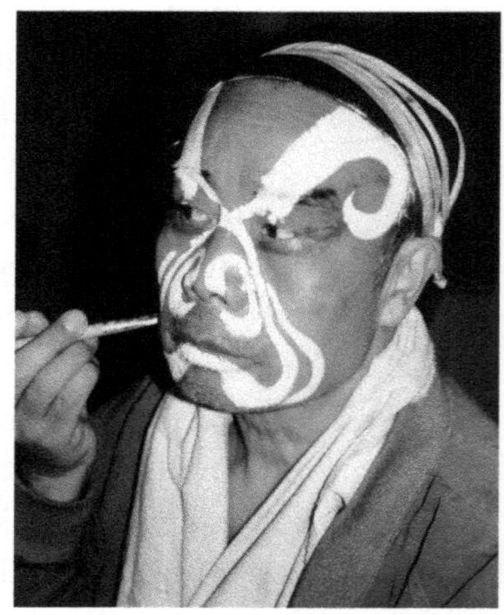

A folk artist putting on make-up for the folk play "Mu Lian rescuing his mother."

Lanterns floating on the river at Ullam-bana Festival in the ancient city of Shanghai

People in Keelung, Taiwan, set fire to paper money in a memorial ceremony for their ancestors in the Ghost Festival.

are lit on the land, while lanterns in *Zhongyuan* are lit on the river. All the shops will also be closed to make way for the ghosts. In the middle of every street there will be a table to place fresh fruit and "ghosts' bread" every hundred paces, with Taoists singing obscure "songs for ghosts." This ceremony is called *Shiger*.

This festival is not very common today, and only appears in some grand ceremonies in monasteries. However, it developed greatly in Japan and has become second only to the New Year Festival there.

Mid-Autumn Festival

Name: Mid-Autumn Festival
Date: the fifteenth day of the eighth lunar month

According to the Chinese lunar calendar, the seventh, eighth and ninth lunar months make up autumn. The eighth lunar month is in the middle of autumn, and the fifteenth of the eighth month is in the middle of this month, so the festival is called "Mid-Autumn Festival." At this time it is usually clear and cool and there are seldom clouds in the sky, so the moon is particularly bright and clear at night. It is on the night of the fifteenth day in the eighth lunar month that the moon is full, so that is the best time for people to enjoy the moon. The full moon is considered a symbol of reunion; therefore Mid-Autumn Festival is also called "the Reunion Festival," and is second only to the Spring Festival in importance.

The Mid-Autumn Festival has had a long history, and offering sacrifices to the moon and enjoying the moonlight were very important customs. The ancient kings offered sacrifices to the sun in spring and to the moon in autumn. This was also practiced by the people. Celebrating the moon became more popular, and the serious ceremony of worship turned into light-hearted entertainment. Celebrating the moon on Mid-Autumn Festival was very popular in the Tang Dynasty and some distinguished poets wrote poems about the moon. Moon-related activities became even more widespread in the Song, Ming and Qing dynasties, and the "Praying-to-Moon Altar," the "Praying-to-Moon Summerhouse" and the "Observing Moon Tower" still

The Mid-Autumn Festival Evening Party on CCTV in 2005.

survive today. The "Moon Altar" in Beijing was built for the royal families to offer sacrifices to the moon in the Jiajing period of the Ming Dynasty (1521–67). Instead of sacrifices, people now enjoy colorful activities with family and friends. Like eating *zongzi* during the Dragon Boat Festival and eating *tangyuan* on the Lantern Festival, eating moon cakes is essential on Mid-Autumn Festival. The moon cake is round, which signifies reunion (*tuanyuan*: in Chinese "round" is *yuan*), so it is also called *tuanyuan* cake in some places. Throughout history the moon cake has always been regarded as a symbol of good luck and happy reunion. Every Mid-Autumn Festival, the whole family will get together and celebrate, eating moon cakes, enjoying the bright moon and chatting. This has a long history in China. One version of its origin records that when Emperor Taizong of Tang (r. 626–649) was in power, General Li Jing (571–649) returned from his victory against the Xiongnu (an ancient ethnic group in the north of China) on the fifteenth day of the eighth lunar month. At that time a businessman from Turpan (a place in northwestern China) offered some cakes to the king to celebrate the victory. Taizong took out the round cake and pointed to the moon with a smile, "I'd like to invite the toad [in Chinese culture the toad represents the moon] to enjoy the *Hu* cake" (that is, cake from *Hu* people, the word that people of the Han nationality used to describe other ethnic groups in ancient China). Then he shared the cakes with the ministers. Since then the custom of eating *Hu* cakes spread all over the country. Another legend goes that the later Emperor Xuanzong of Tang (r. 712–756) had once enjoyed the moon and eaten *Hu* cakes with his favorite, Concubine Yang (719–756). Li did not like the name of *Hu* cake, so Concubine Yang looked at the moon and said, "Why not call it moon cake?"

Moon cakes.

There are many types of moon cakes in China, and the recipes vary between different areas. There are five main types, from Beijing, Tianjin, Guangzhou, Suzhou and Chaozhou, each with its own specialty. The stuffing of moon cakes is either sweet or savory; either meat or fruit. They are decorated prettily with flower patterns and Chinese characters, making them attractive as well as delicious.

The poem *In the Still of the Night* written by the great poet Li Bai (701–762) in the Tang Dynasty is so famous among the Chinese that even young children can recite it:

I see bright moonlight in front of my bed.
It looks like hoar frost on the floor.
I look up and see the bright moon,
I bow my head and miss my homeland.

The poem expresses the feelings of those who are away from home on Mid-Autumn Festival. They cannot spend the holiday with their families and so can only enjoy the bright moon symbolizing happiness and reunion and express good wishes to the moonlight.

Since ancient times there have been many legends and stories about the moon in China, the most famous of which is "Chang E's flight to the moon." Chang E was the wife of Hou Yi, the hero who shot down nine suns in the ancient Chinese legend. It is said that she ate the elixir of life given by the Queen Mother of the Western

"Chang E" by Wu Youru, late Qing Dynasty.

Heavens without her husband's permission. She turned into a goddess and flew to the moon. It is said that if you look carefully, you can see the jade rabbit, legendary companion to Chang E, on the moon on Mid-Autumn Festival. A second legend is the story of "Wu Gang cutting the laurel." Wu Gang sought immortality and became a god, but was exiled to the moon for some mistake and was ordered to cut the laurel in front of the *Guanghan* Palace (the palace on the moon) every day. The laurel was over five hundred *zhang* high (a *zhang* is a third of a meter), and whenever Wu managed to cut into the tree, it would heal instantly. So he had to repeat the hard work forever in vain. All these legends add mystery and romance to the moon, and children still like to hear these stories from their parents when watching the moon.

There is a one-day holiday on the Mid-Autumn Festival.

Double Ninth Festival

Name: Double Ninth Festival
Date: the ninth day of the ninth lunar month

The ninth day of the ninth lunar month is the "Double Ninth Festival" in China. In the ancient Chinese book *Yijing* (or *I-Ching, The Book of Changes*), six was seen as the *yin* number, while nine was the *yang* number. The ninth day of the ninth lunar month includes two yang numbers, so the day is called Double *Yang* or "Double Nine." The earliest record of the name of "Double Ninth Festival" dates to the period of Three Kingdoms (220–280).

The origin of Double Ninth Festival dates back to at least the beginning of the Han Dynasty. At that time, Empress Lü Zhi was so jealous of Concubine Qi, one of the favorites of Emperor Gao (the first emperor of the Han Dynasty, 256 or 247–195 BC), that she ill-treated her and drove her maid out of the imperial palace to marry a commoner. This maid, known as Miss Jia, told people that in the imperial palace, every ninth day of the ninth lunar

month, they wore dogwood and drank chrysanthemum wine to ward off disaster. Many common people followed the custom and it gradually spread all over the country.

The custom of wearing dogwood was already very popular in the Tang Dynasty. Dogwood is a heavily-scented plant with edible fruit. The infusion and leaves have medicinal properties. They can expel insects, lessen humidity, help digestion and cure fever. The ancient Chinese believed that planting dogwood on Double Ninth Festival could prevent diseases and avoid disasters. They also wore dogwood on their arms or heads or put it in sachets. The custom is mainly followed by women and children, but in some places men also wear it.

Besides dogwood, chrysanthemums are also worn by people on Double Ninth Festival. Chrysanthemums bloom in the ninth lunar month and they have the beautiful name "flower of longevity." The custom of wearing chrysanthemums had already appeared in the Tang Dynasty and has been very popular ever since. In the Qing Dynasty, people in Beijing began to attach chrysanthemums to doors and windows to "get rid of bad luck and bring in good." It is always bright and clear around Double Ninth Festival and the chrysanthemums are in bloom then, so drinking wine while enjoying chrysanthemums is also one of the traditional customs of this festival. Enjoying chrysanthemums and drinking

Chrysanthemum party.

chrysanthemum wine originated in the Eastern Jin Dynasty (317–420) when the great poet Tao Yuanming (365–427) lived. Tao was famous for his reclusive life in the countryside, his excellence as a poet, and his fondness for wine and also chrysanthemums. Other people imitated him and the custom spread. Scholar officials then added feasting to enjoying chrysanthemums in order to be more like Tao Yuanming. This custom spread in the capital Kaifeng in the Song Dynasty. After the Qing Dynasty, this custom became even more popular, and not limited to the ninth day of the ninth lunar month. But the grandest celebrations, of course, are still around the Double Ninth Festival when the air is crisp, the sky is clear and chrysanthemums are in bloom everywhere.

"Tao Yuanming Enjoying Chrysanthemums" by Jiang Zhaohe.

Later, the custom of eating "Double Ninth cakes" became popular. Double Ninth cake is made of flour, with jujubes, gingkoes apricots and pine nuts added to make it sweet, or meat to make it savory. Some special Double Ninth cakes have nine layers and look like a tower. There should be two little sheep on the top, which is to go with the "double *yang*" (the word for sheep in Chinese is *yang*).

Traditionally, people also like to climb mountains on this festival, so Double Ninth Festival is also called "Mountain-climbing Festival." At this bright and clear time in autumn it is a real pleasure to climb mountains and enjoy the beauty of nature. Climbing mountains on Double Ninth Festival was already common in the Tang Dynasty, and there are many poems about it, such as *On the Ninth Day of the Ninth Lunar Festival: Thinking of My Brothers in Shandong* written by the great poet Wang Wei during the Tang Dynasty:

All alone in a foreign land,
I am twice as homesick on this day.
When my brothers carry dogwood up the mountain,
Each of them a branch, and my branch missing.

As well as being believed to prevent bad luck and disasters, climbing mountains also suggests "climbing to a higher position," and this is another important reason why people used to follow this custom. Another reason that climbing mountains is popular, especially with the elderly, is that it has the implication of "climbing to a longer life" leading them to hope to live longer

The custom of planting dogwood on Double Ninth Festival is no longer followed, but many people still climb mountains, enjoy chrysanthemums and appreciate the beautiful scenery of autumn. In recent years a new aspect has been added to the old festival

Older people enjoying chrysanthemums in a park on Double Ninth Festival.

and it has become an annual "Respect-the-Senior Festival." On this day, people will hold all kinds of activities to express their good wishes to older people for their health and happiness

Dong Jie

Name: *Dong Jie* (Winter Solstice)
Date: the seasonal division point Winter Solstice (December 22 or 23)

Winter Solstice, commonly known as *Dong Jie*, was a very important festival in ancient times. With daylight at its shortest in the northern hemisphere on that day, and night at its longest, it is the coldest day in the year. This day is also the turning point between winter and spring. Thus among the twenty-four seasonal divisions, Winter Solstice is the most important.

The ancient people believed that when Winter Solstice came, though it was still cold, spring was just around the corner. People who were away from home should return to show that they had reached their destination at the end of the year. In Fujian and Taiwan, Winter Solstice is regarded as the day of family reunions: they offer sacrifices to their ancestors, and anyone who does not return home will be seen as someone who has forgotten their ancestors.

The night of the Winter Solstice is the longest in the year; many families will take advantage of this to make "Winter Solstice dumplings" of glutinous rice. To distinguish the day from *ci sui* (farewell to the outgoing year) on the lunar New Year's Eve, the day before Winter Solstice is named *tian sui* or *a sui* suggesting that although the calendar year (in Chinese *sui* means year) has not yet ended, everyone is a year older.

Winter Solstice dumplings are always kneaded into the shape of little animals such as cats, dogs, rabbits and tigers, as chosen by children, which they always enjoy. Before eating the Winter

Solstice dumplings, people should put a dumpling behind each door, window, table, cupboard and light. These dumplings are called *hao shang* and can only be baked and eaten after a ritualistic "farewell dinner" is offered to the Kitchen God. It is said that if any woman in the family is pregnant at that time, she will give birth to a boy if the dumplings expand; if not it will be a girl. For good luck, the number of people eating Winter Solstice dumplings should be even. At the end of the feast, if there are two dumplings left, any married guests will get what they want in the future; while if there is only one left, the single ones will lead the life they wish. Some families also offer sacrifices to gods and their ancestors with some seasonal fruits and meat. People may also follow the tradition of putting winter rice in the sun, which involves washing the rice with water, putting it in the sun and finally putting it away to be made into porridge for anyone who may get ill in the future.

"The cold will pass in eighty-one days," New Year poster. After the Winter Solstice, people welcome bright and beautiful spring through eighty-one cold days. This kind of poster would be used as a calendar and a form of decoration.

Statutory Festivals

There are three kinds of statutory Chinese festivals and memorial days. On the first kind, all citizens are entitled to a holiday, including New Year's Day (one-day holiday), Spring Festival (three-day holiday), Labor Day (three-day holiday) and National Day (three-day holiday). The second type of festival concerns just a certain group of people, including Women's Day (half-day holiday only for women), Youth Day (half-day holiday for young people over fourteen years old), Children's Day (one-day holiday for those under thirteen years old) and Army Day (half-day holiday for soldiers in active service). The third type does not involve a holiday. These include: July 1 Memorial Day for the establishment of the Chinese Communist Party, July 7 Memorial Day for the beginning of the anti-Japanese War, September 3 Memorial Day for the victory in the anti-Japanese War, Tree-Planting Day, Teachers' Day, Nurses' Day, Journalists' Day and so on.

New Year's Day

Name: New Year's Day (*Yuan Dan* in Chinese)
Date: January 1

The concept of *Nian* (meaning "year" in Chinese) originally derived from agricultural production. In ancient times, people regarded the growth cycle of grain as *Nian*, or a year. During the Xia Dynasty (2070–1600 BC) and the Shang Dynasty (1600–1046 BC), the Chinese developed the Xia Calendar. This took the cycle of the moon as a month and divided a year into twelve months. Chinese people usually call the first day of a year *Yuan Dan*. *Yuan* means "beginning," and *Dan* is daybreak, also meaning daytime. The combination of *Yuan* and *Dan* means the very beginning, namely the first day of the year.

Originally, the first day of *Zheng Yue* (the first lunar month) was called *Yuan Dan* in China, but there was no common agreement which day should be the first day of *Zheng Yue*. The dates of the Chinese New Year's Day also varied between various dynasties. For instance, it fell on the first day of *Zheng Yue* in the Xia Dynasty, on the first day of the twelfth lunar month in the Shang Dynasty, and on the first day of the eleventh lunar month in the Zhou Dynasty. After Qin Shihuang (the first emperor of China, 259–210 BC) unified the six states, the Qin Dynasty took the first day of the tenth lunar month as *Yuan Dan*, and this was followed by the later dynasties. In 104 BC, Emperor Wu of Han (r. 141–87 BC) accepted the advice

On New Year's Eve people strike a bell and pray for a happy New Year.

An enormous "Chinese knot."

of Sima Qian (born around 140 BC) and others and began to use the *Taichu* Calendar, which is the Chinese lunar calendar still in use today. Like the calendar of the Xia Dynasty, the *Taichu* Calendar also took *Zheng Yue* as the beginning of the year, and adopted the twenty-four solar periods. Although all the later dynasties made some changes, they basically followed this system and took the first day of *Zheng Yue* as *Yuan Dan*.

After the Xinhai Revolution in 1911, the government of the Qing Dynasty was overthrown, the feudal rule of China was abolished, and Sun Zhongshan (or Sun Yat-sen, 1866–1925) established the government of the Republic of China (1912–1949) in Nanjing. The representatives of all provincial

Annual New Year Concerts are becoming the fashion in many cities.

governors gathered in Nanjing to discuss the problem of the calendar. In order to be convenient for agricultural production and for statistics, the government stipulated that the lunar calendar would be used in daily life, and the Gregorian calendar would be used in government, factories, schools and social organizations. On September 27, 1949, the first session of the Chinese People's Political Consultation Conference (CPPCC) passed a resolution, declaring January 1 of the Gregorian calendar as *Yuan Dan* (namely New Year's Day) and the first day of the lunar calendar as *Chun Jie* (namely Spring Festival, also called the New Year's Day of the lunar calendar).

Chinese people attach more importance to the New Year's Day of the lunar calendar than to that of the Gregorian Calendar. The festivities for New Year's Day, therefore, are on a smaller scale than those of *Chun Jie*. However, around New Year's Day there are large-scale celebrations, such as orchestral concerts and parties. Greetings cards are also exchanged among friends, relatives and some organizations to express good wishes.

March 8 Women's Day

Name: International Labor Women's Day
Date: March 8

International Labor Women's Day, also called "the UN Day for Women's Rights and International Peace" or "March 8 Day," is a holiday to commemorate the struggle of women throughout the world for peace, democracy and liberation.

On March 8, 1857, female workers in the clothes and textile factories of New York held a demonstration to protest against inhumane working environments, the twelve-hour working day

and low pay. The demonstration was broken up by the police. Two years later, again in March, these women organized their first trade union.

On March 8, 1908, 1,500 women marched in New York City and asked for shorter working hours, better pay, the right to vote, and a ban on child labor. Their slogan was "Bread and Roses," where bread symbolized economic security and roses a better quality of life.

On March 8, 1909, female workers in Chicago went on a major strike and held a demonstration. They demanded increased wages, an eight-hour working day and the right to vote.

In March 1910, the Second International Conference of Socialist Women from seventeen countries was held in Copenhagen, Denmark. They discussed important issues such as opposing armaments, protecting children's rights,

Beautifully dressed women of various nationalities gather to celebrate the March Eighth Festival in front of the gate of the Great Hall of the People.

campaigning for the eight-hour day, women's right to vote and so on. Clara Zetkin, a German socialist revolutionary and a leader of the international women's movement, suggested March 8 as the International Day of Women's Struggle so as to unite all working women throughout the world to oppose imperialistic wars, oppression, and to struggle for women's rights and liberation. This proposal was agreed unanimously at this conference, and March 8 became International Labor Women's Day.

A wife is touched by her husband's surprise message. The text on the board reads: "Happy Women's Day! I love you! Thank you for your dedication!"

In China, celebrations were held for the first time in 1924 to commemorate International Labor Women's Day. Led by the famous female activist He Xiangning (1878–1972), Chinese women from all walks of life gathered in Guangzhou to commemorate this Women's Day. Amongst their slogans were "Down with imperialistic warlords," "Abolish polygamy," "Ban concubinage," which suggested their opposition to imperialism and the feudal system, and their determination to champion women's rights. From then on, celebrations were held every year on that day. After the foundation of the People's Republic of China, the central government decreed that March 8 every year would be a festival of Chinese women. On that day all women enjoy a half-day holiday, with other celebrations and activities.

1n 1977, the thirty-second UN Congress formally determined March 8 as "the UN Day for Women's Rights and International Peace."

Tree-Planting Day

Name: Chinese Tree-Planting Day
Date: March 12

Portrait of Sun Yat-sen.

Tree-Planting Day is a statutory festival held in some countries to encourage the planting and protection of trees, to increase forestation, and to protect the natural environment.

The US State of Nebraska is where Tree-Planting Day first originated. On April 10, 1872, Sterling Morton, a famous American agriculturist, proposed the establishment of a Tree-Planting Day at a meeting of the Garden Society of Nebraska and this was adopted by the State. From 1885, April 22 became the state Tree-Planting Day. Following this, the other states of the US and other countries followed suit.

After the Xinhai Revolution of 1911, Sun Yat-sen, the Chinese leader at that time, put forward a large-scale plan for planting trees in the northern and central parts of China, and announced plans for future agricultural modernization. In 1924, in a speech in Guangzhou, he stressed: "our research findings indicate that the main way to avoid flood and drought is to plant trees and establish forests. We need to have large areas of forests." Later, in his writing and speeches, he stressed again

Beiyang Government
Also called the Beijing Government, a general term for the Republic of China government in Beijing controlled by Northern Warlords from 1912 to 1928. The Warlords in power at this time included Duan Qirui, Feng Guozhang, Wang Shizhen, Cao Kun, Wu Peifu, Zhang Zuolin and Sun Chuanfang. In 1921, the Nationalist Party of China established the National Government in Guangzhou in South China, effectively disuniting China. The Beiyang Government was acknowledged internationally as the official government of the Republic of China until 1928, when it was replaced by the National Government.

Little "gardeners" planting azaleas on Tree-Planting Day.

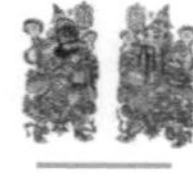

and again the dangers of damaging forests and the importance of planting trees.

In 1915, in response to Sun Yat-sen's proposal, the Beiyang Government (or Northern Government) formally ruled that Pure Brightness Festival (April 5) would become Tree-Planting Day, giving China its own Tree-Planting Festival. But at a later date, the national government decided to take March 12, the date when Sun Yat-sen passed away, as Tree-Planting Day, as Pure Brightness Festival falls at a time which is too late for tree-planting in the southern part of China.

In February 1979, the sixth session of the standing committee of the Fifth National People's Congress resolved that March 12 would be Chinese Tree-Planting Day. This required the whole country to carry out tree-planting activities on this day, and the whole of society to support the construction of forestry. In 1981, at the proposal of Deng Xiaoping (1904–1997), the Fifth National People's Congress passed the *Resolution on Launching a Campaign of Voluntary Tree-Planting throughout the Country.*

When Tree-Planting Day is approaching, people usually go outdoors to fulfill their duty of planting trees. The state leaders often take the lead in planting trees on that day every year. People's awareness of environmental conservation, harmonious development and social responsibility is strengthened by the policy of voluntary tree-planting. Since December 1981, the total number of trees planted voluntarily has reached thirty-five billion.

According to UN statistics, fifty countries so far have established a Tree-Planting Day.

May 1 International Labor Day

Name: International Labor Day
Date: May 1

International Labor Day is the common festival of all the proletarians and working people of the world. It originates from a major strike in the US city of Chicago on May 1, 1886, when 216,000 workers went on strike for an eight-hour working day. They finally won after a hard, bloody fight. To commemorate this great workers' strike, at the Conference for Socialist Representatives held in Paris on July 14, 1889, French representatives proposed that May 1, should be set as a common festival for international proletarians. This was agreed unanimously and on that day International Labor Day was born, supported by workers all over the world. From then on, working people of all countries held rallies and parades on that day every year to celebrate the festival.

In 1918 the Chinese people began to celebrate Labor Day. Campaigners worked to introduce May 1 as Labor Day in

Workers' representatives singing "We Workers Are Powerful."

Telephone cards distributed by CNC (China Netcom) for Labor Day.

Shanghai, Suzhou, Hangzhou, Hankou and various other places. On May 1, 1920, some workers in Beijing, Shanghai, Guangzhou, Jiujiang, Tangshan and other industrial cities held a great rally and parade: the first Labor Day celebration.

After the foundation of the People's Republic of China, the central government set May 1 as a statutory festival in December 1949, and declared it a one-day holiday. People dressed up for the festival and gathered in parks, theatres and squares for various celebrations and entertainments. Working people who had made outstanding contributions would be rewarded on that day. On September 18, 1999, the State Council increased the holiday to three days and from 2000, the total holiday became seven days (the statutory three-day holiday plus the two weekends before and after May 1).

May 4 Youth Day

Name: Chinese Youth Day
Date: May 4

Chinese Youth Day originated with the May Fourth Movement, the anti-imperialist and patriotic movement which swept China in 1919.

In 1919, following the end of the First World War, the UK, France, the US, Japan, Italy and other countries held the Versailles Peace Conference. The Chinese government of the time sent some representatives to the conference, and demanded that the imperial countries should abandon their privilege in China, that Japan should cancel the "Twenty-one Demands," a treaty imposed on China by Japan, and that China should regain sovereignty over Shandong, which was occupied by Germany before the war and by Japan during the war. In May 1919, the Versailles Conference refused

China's request to abolish the "Twenty-one Demands," and even decided to transfer Germany's privileges in Shandong Province to Japan. There was great anger at this news in China. On May 4, about 3,000 students from various universities in Beijing gathered in Tian'anmen Square and held a student protest march for the first time in Chinese history. The students' patriotic slogans included "sovereignty abroad and punishing national traitors at home," "cancel the twenty-one-demand treaty" and "refuse to sign the so-called peace treaty." They presented a petition to the state president which was suppressed by the warlord government of the time, causing more anger. Many students, workers and others went on strike, and the students' demonstration and parade finally developed into a national anti-imperialist patriotic movement. On June 10, the warlord government had to compromise, and deposed Cao Rulin, Zhang Zongxiang and Lu Zongyu, who were regarded as traitors. On June 28 Chinese representatives at the Versailles Conference refused to sign the Peace Treaty. The news spread abroad quickly and the imperialist powers were shocked. At that point, the Movement's main goals had been largely achieved.

The May Fourth Movement is a landmark event in Chinese history. It was not only a patriotic student movement, but also a new cultural movement promoting democracy and science over feudal culture, and resulting later in the adoption of the modern Chinese language.

The May Fourth Movement.

The May Fourth Movement reflected the strong will of the Chinese people to preserve national independence and strive for democracy and freedom.

Students take an oath and release a red balloon in the adulthood ceremony.

In order to pass on and extend the spirit of the May Fourth Movement, the Chinese government formally stated in 1949 that May 4 would be Chinese Youth Day. On this festival, a variety of celebrations are held all over the country, such as rallies, voluntary activities, social events and some ceremonies for those reaching adulthood.

On Youth Day, all young people in the country over fourteen years old have a half-day holiday.

June 1 International Children's Day

Name: International Children's Day
Date: June 1

Children's Day is a festival for children all over the world. In August 1925, representatives from fifty-four countries gathered in Geneva, Switzerland, to hold the World Conference for the Well-being of Children, and produced a document, the *Geneva*

Manifesto for Safeguarding Children. This covered the spiritual guidance of children, the relief of child poverty, the avoidance of dangerous work for children, preparation for employment, education and so on. Since this conference, the governments of many countries have established a "Children's Day," to inspire and entertain children and to draw attention to child-protection issues.

The international festival originated in the Second World War. In June 1942, German soldiers shot around 140 male villagers over sixteen and all of the babies in a village in Czechoslovakia, and took all the women and ninety children to a concentration camp.

In remembrance of all the children who died in this village and all over the world during the Second World War, and in support of children's right to survival, health care and education, the International Democratic Society of Women held a conference of its executive committee in Moscow in November 1949, and formally resolved that June 1 every year would be a festival for children all over the world, namely Children's Day.

Since 1931, April 4 had been Children's Day in China. After the foundation of the PRC, in 1949, June 1 was declared to be the Children's Day of the New China.

Today, governments of all countries have regard for children's rights. In 1990, the UN passed the *Convention on the Rights of the Child*, and China was one of the countries participating in drafting and signing the agreement. In the

Children work together to paint a picture one hundred meters long on Children's Day.

Children enjoying a party.

same year the government ratified the *Convention on the Rights of the Child* and enacted the *Law for Protecting Minors of the People's Republic of China*, which played an active role in safeguarding children's rights. Children now have a good standard of living, education and health care. On June 1 all children under the age of thirteen years have a one-day holiday and in some places their parents can also enjoy the one-day holiday. As "little super stars" for the day, children usually go with their parents to parks, zoos, pleasure grounds, visit science and technology exhibitions, museums and planetariums, or take part in specialized activities such as competitions for Chinese calligraphy and drawings in children's activity centers. Children greatly enjoy this festival of their own.

August 1 Army's Day

Name: Army's Day (Memorial Day for the Foundation of PLA of China)
Date: August 1

August 1 is the Memorial Day for the foundation of People's Liberation Army of the PRC.

At the beginning of the democratic revolution, led by Sun Yat-sen, the Chinese Communist Party (CCP) and the Chinese Kuomintang were allied. In April 1927, Chiang Kai-shek (1887–1975) of the Kuomintang launched a violent anti-revolutionary *coup d'etat*, bringing to an end the cooperation between the Chinese Communist Party and Chinese Kuomintang. In order to save the revolution, about 20,000 members of the northern expedition army, who were influenced by the CCP, led by Zhou Enlai (1898–1976), He Long (1896–1969), Ye Ting

Honor Guards of the Chinese People's Liberation Army.

The Nanchang Uprising, a relief on the Monument of the People's Heroes in Tian'anmen Square, Beijing.

(1896–1946), Zhu De (1886–1976) and Liu Bocheng (1892–1986), started an uprising in Nanchang, Jiangxi Province, on August 1 of that year. This was a parting shot to the rulers of the Kuomintang, and marked the point at which the Chinese Communist Party began to lead the armed revolution on its own. Shortly after the uprising the army took over Nanchang city, marched toward the southern Guangdong Province, and was finally dispersed by the enemy. A part of the army led by Zhu De and Chen Yi (1901–1972) arrived at the Jinggangshan Mountain of Jiangxi Province in April 1928, joined forces with the army led by Mao Zedong (1893–1976), and formed the Chinese Red Army, mainly consisting of workers and peasants and led by the Chinese Communist Party (CCP). Through the Long March, Anti-Japanese War and Liberation War, this army got stronger, and finally became today's People's Liberation Army of China.

On June 26, 1933, the CCP resolved that August 1 would be set as a memorial day for the establishment of the Chinese Red Army. On June 30, 1933, the central military committee of the Red Army announced: "On August 1, 1927, the Nanchang Insurrection, led by a proletariat party, the CCP, took place. This insurrection was the beginning of the Land Revolution against imperialism, and the source of the valiant Red Army." On July 11 the central authority organization of the revolutionary base area – the Interim Government of the Chinese Soviet Republic – ratified the proposal that August 1 be adopted as the Army Day. Since then, around August 1, various activities supporting the army and their relatives take place.

The Nanchang Uprising Monument, Nanchang, Jiangxi.

After the foundation of Chinese People's Liberation Army, August 1 remained as Army Day.

Teachers' Day

Name: Chinese Teachers' Day
Date: September 10

Teachers' Day is one of the three occupational festivals in China, the other two being Nurses' Day and Journalists' Day. Between 1931 and the present day there have been Teachers' Days in China on various dates. The first Teachers' Day was in 1931. The well-known professors Tai Shuangqiu and Cheng

Qibao set June 6 as Teachers' Day, and published the *Manifesto on Teachers' Day* with three goals – improving teachers' standard of living, safeguarding their employment and improving their skills. The Kuomintang government in power at the time objected, but the movement did have some influence throughout the country.

In 1939, the Kuomintang government decided to set August 27, the birthday of the ancient Chinese scholar Confucius, as Teachers' Day, and issued regulations to this effect, but it was not widely supported.

In 1951, the Ministry of Education and the All-China Federation of Trade Unions made a resolution that May 1 International Labor Day was also determined as Teachers' Day. Since teachers did not have their own celebrations on this day, this Teachers' Day also did not attract much attention.

On December 9 1984, Professor Wang Zikun, President of Beijing Normal University, once again came up with the idea that "teachers should have their own festival," and contacted the *Beijing Evening Paper*. The next day, the *Beijing Evening Paper* published an article reporting Professor Wang Zikun's ideas for activities to honor teachers and highlight education, which provoked a strong response. On December 15, professors Zhong Jingwen, Qi Gong, Wang Zikun, Tao Dayong, Zhu Zhixian, Huang Ji, Zhao Qinghuan and others from Beijing Normal University formally proposed that Teachers' Day should be set. To maintain and develop the tradition of "respecting teachers and attaching importance to education," and in order to raise the status of teachers, the ninth session

Portrait of Confucius.

of the standing committee of the sixth NPC resolved on January 21, 1985, that September 10 would be set as Teachers' Day.

Kindergarten children painting a colored dress for their teacher.

Teachers' Day is the date on which students in primary schools, middle schools, colleges and universities start their new terms. With the start of the new term, students sense the atmosphere of respect for teachers and the importance of education, promoting good relationships between teachers and students. September 10 1985 was the first Teachers' Day after its reintroduction. President Li Xiannian (1909–1992) wrote a letter of greeting to all the teachers of the country. In Beijing, 10,000 people gathered to hold a celebration conference. During the festival, 11,871 teaching groups and individual teachers were awarded prizes in twenty provinces. Chinese teachers now had their own unique festival.

National Day

Name: National Day
Date: October 1

At three o'clock on October 1, 1949, 300,000 people held a ceremony in Tian'anmen Square to celebrate the founding of the People's Central Government of the PRC. Chairman Mao Zedong solemnly declared the founding of the People's Central Government and of the PRC and personally hoisted the first five-star flag. He read out the following *Announcement of the People's Central Government of the PRC*: "The People's Central Government of the PRC is the only legal government to stand for all people of the PRC. Our government is willing to establish a diplomatic relationship with any foreign government that agrees to abide by the principles of equality, mutual benefit, mutual respect for territorial integrity and so on." There was then a parade and folk procession. Zhu De – Commander in Chief – inspected the forces and announced the *Order of the Chinese People's Liberation Army Headquarters*, ordering the army to clear all remaining armed forces of Kuomintang reactionaries and to liberate all unfree land. On the same day, the Beijing Xinhua broadcasting station broadcast the founding ceremony of the PRC live from Tian'anmen Square, the first large-scale live broadcast in China, with simultaneous broadcasts all over China.

At the first meeting of the first session of the national committee of the Chinese People's Political Consultative Conference, a representative said "the founding of the PRC should have a day for celebration. So I hope this session will set October 1 as a national holiday." Mao Zedong replied, "We have to let the government decide." On December 3, 1949, the fourth session of the People's Central Government committee passed a resolution stating that October 1, the day when the founding of the PRC had been announced, would be a national holiday every year. From 1950 this has been a day of great celebration for all nationalities in China.

Before 1970, as a major part of the celebration, a state banquet, military parade, fireworks and procession were held every year. There were large meetings in Tian'anmen Square as well as in all provinces, regions and counties. At these meetings not only leaders of all levels but also workers, farmers and representatives from the liberation army made speeches, expressing the love of

On October 1, 1949, Chairman Mao Zedong solemnly announced to the world that the new China had been founded.

people of all walks of life for the PRC. After the meeting there was usually a parade. Excited people would wave brightly colored triangular flags and shout slogans parading through the streets.

When the New China was founded, the PRC Political Consultative Committee decided to include a military parade as a major element in the national holiday ceremony. On the sixty national days from the founding ceremony to 2009, fourteen military parades were held.

In 1960, the government decided to have "a minor celebration every five years and major celebration every ten years with military parades" to conserve public funds for other uses. On the twentieth national holiday in 1969, although it was a major celebration, no military parade was held, on account of the problem of deploying forces and constraints on national finances. The year 1979 was the thirtieth anniversary, but reform and opening up had just started and recovery and reconstruction was in hand, so no military parade was held then either. However, the government held a state banquet for 4,000 people and all the major parks held activities. Until 1984, China had not held military parades on national holidays for twenty-four years. In that year, at the suggestion of Deng Xiaoping, who was then the national leader, the Chinese government decided to resume the military parade and held a large-scale military parade ceremony at Tian'anmen Square that year, the thirty-fifth anniversary of the founding of the PRC.

At the end of August 2004, the Chinese government made new arrangements for the national holiday. This was the third time

The flag-raising ceremony in Tian'anmen Square.

that the government had asked to celebrate in an economical way after the founding of New China. In that year, the major arrangements for the national holiday in Beijing included a reception banquet, a large-scale theatrical evening in celebration of the fifty-fifth anniversary of the PRC, themed activities celebrating patriotism and revolutionary traditions for young people and so on.

On October 1, 2009, the sixtieth anniversary of the founding of the PRC, a grand ceremony, a solemn military review and a mass parade were held at Tian'anmen Square in Beijing.

Since 2000, the national holiday lasts seven days. The Chinese economy is growing all the time, so people have more choice for relaxation and recreation. More and more people choose to go on trips, going abroad to South-east Asia, Europe, North America and Japan for holidays. The National holiday, Spring Festival and May Day holiday combine so

A huge floral basket in Tian'anmen Square during National Day holiday 2009.

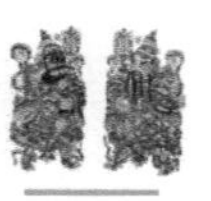

Crowds on the Great Wall during the National Day "Golden travel week."

that the three major "golden weeks for tourism" can merge. This has also boosted the new "holiday economy" of tourism, transportation, the telecoms industry, the gift industry and the catering trade.

Smiling girls at Tian'anmen Gate during National Day holiday 2009.

Festivals of the Chinese People

China is a united multi-ethnic state. To date, fifty-six ethnic groups have been identified by the Chinese government. Since the Han Chinese represent ninety-two percent of the whole population, China's other fifty-five ethnic groups are often referred to as the national minorities.

These groups include Mongolian, Hui, Tibetan, Uygur, Miao, Yi, Zhuang, Bouyei, Korean, Manchu, Dong, Yao, Bai, Tujia, Hani, Kazak, Dai, Li, Lisu, Va, She, Gaoshan, Lahu, Shui, Dongxiang, Naxi, Jingpo, Kirgiz, Tu, Daur, Mulam, Qiang, Blang, Salar, Maonan, Gelao, Xibe, Achang, Pumi, Tajik, Nu, Ozbek, Russian, Ewenki, De'ang, Bonan, Yugur, Jing, Tatar, Drung, Oroqen, Hezhen, Moinba, Lhoba and Jino.

Among them, Zhuang, the largest group, has more than 15 million people, followed by Manchu, Hui, Uygur, Miao, Yi, Tujia, Mongolian, Tibetan, Bouyei, Dong, Yao, Korean, Bai, Hani, Kazak, Li and Dai, each having a population of more than one million. However, there are only a few thousand people in ethnic groups such as Ewenki and Oroqen.

The Han people are found in all parts of the country, but mainly in the middle and lower reaches of the Yellow River, Yangtze River, Pearl River and the Northeast Plain. Most of the non-Han ethnic groups live in the border regions in the Northeast, Southwest and Northwest, but others are found all over China. In many parts of China, ethnic groups including the Han live together.

The Han people have their own spoken and written language, commonly known as the Chinese language, which is used throughout China and is one of the six working languages of the United Nations. The Hui and Manchu ethnic groups also use the Han Chinese language. However, a total of fifty-three ethnic groups use spoken languages of their own, while twenty-three ethnic groups have their own written languages.

Each ethnic group in China has its own long history and unique culture. They have different lifestyles, customs and habits. The clothes they wear, the food they eat, the houses they build, and the wedding ceremonies and funerals they hold differ from one to another. The traditions of these ethnic groups are highly respected and they have the right to maintain and develop their own traditions and to celebrate them as they wish.

Naturally, different people in China celebrate various festivals and almost every nationality has their own major festival. Typical examples are the Tibetan New Year, the Water-Splashing Festival for Dai people, and the Torch Festival for the Yi people, the Singing Carnival for the Zhuang people and the *Nadam* Fair for the Mongolians.

Nadam Fair

Name: *Nadam* Fair of the Mongolians
Date: between July and August

In Mongolian, *nadam* means recreation or game. The traditional annual festival is a grand gathering of the Mongolian people during the golden period between July and August when the grass on the meadows is ripe and the livestock is in the best physical condition for cattle-trading. The main events of a *Nadam* Fair are horseracing, wrestling and archery, as well as theatrical performances. To the Mongolian people, the *Nadam* Fair is ancient, sacred, grand and full of fun. Today, it has become a large-scale gathering including sacrificial rites, celebrations, athletic sports, entertainment and trade. Agricultural produce, ethnic crafts and animal products from different areas are exchanged at the fair.

Most Mongolian people live in Inner Mongolia, Gansu, Qinghai, Xinjiang, Jilin and Liaoning. According to the fifth national census in 2000, there are 5,813,900 Mongolians across China. They have their own spoken and written language, which belongs to the Mongolian group of the Altaic language family. The Mongolians use three dialects: Inner Mongolian, Barag-Buryat and Uirad. The Mongolian script was created in the early thirteenth century on the basis of the script of Huihu or ancient Uygur, which was revised and developed a century later into the form used to this day.

In 1206, Temujin (1162–1227) of the Mongolian tribe held a clan conference on the bank of the Onon River, where he was elected the Great Khan of all Mongols with the title of Genghis Khan. Between 1219 and 1260, the Mongolian army launched three massive expeditions, expanding the Mongolian empire into Central Asia and Europe. Genghis Khan died in 1227. In 1272,

Dramatic horse racing during the Nadam Fair.

following more than seventy years of battles, his son Kublai Khan (1215–1294) founded the Yuan Dynasty. In 1276, Kublai Khan subdued the Southern Song, bringing the whole of China under his centralized rule.

As early as the beginning of the thirteenth century, Mongolian tribe chiefs began holding a large gathering called *Nadam*. Records show that after conquering the Khwarezmian Empire in

1220, Genghis Khan held a grand *Nadam* Fair focusing on archery. The *Nadam* Fair then became a regular major event including archery, horseracing and wrestling, which are commonly known among Mongolians as the Three Arts. During the Qing Dynasty, the *Nadam* Fair was held either once every six months or every two years. The winners received horses, camels, cattle, sheep, brick tea or silk.

In the past, large-scale sacrificial rites were held at the beginning of a *Nadam* Fair, with tribal elders or local officials reciting eulogies. Nowadays, sacrificial rites have been reduced to a symbolic opening ceremony, even in the Hinggan area in eastern Inner Mongolia where the *Nadam* Fair retains a very traditional style.

In addition to cattle-trading, celebrating the harvest and praying for a happy and prosperous life, the *Nadam* Fair is a contest of the three ancient nomadic arts of wrestling, archery and horse racing.

Wrestling: the most popular and widespread sport amongst the Mongolians. In ancient times, wrestling champions were hailed as heroes on the pastures and were often chosen

Mongolian wrestling.

Oboo Ritual

"Oboo," refers to the man-made stone piles, usually constructed on top of the hills or highlands of the prairies, which can be found everywhere on the Mongolian prairie functioning as road signs or boundary markers.

The Oboo ritual ceremony has a long history and nowadays has become an act of worship of the mountain god and the road god, praying for blessings from heaven, the prosperity of villagers and livestock, and a safe journey. The people taking part in the sacrifice ceremony must walk around the Oboo three times clockwise, and scatter sacrifices, such as milk, wine, butter and sugar.

by nobles to marry their daughters. For the Mongolian people, wrestling involves both strength and skill.

Usually, wrestlers at a *Nadam* Fair will wear a tight leather vest decorated with silver buttons and knee-high boots, with a necklace of red, yellow and blue ribbons. They enter the arena performing the "eagle dance" and singing loud battle songs. The scene is unforgettable.

Archery: Ancient Mongolians used bows and arrows for hunting and fighting. Indeed, it was bands of skilled archers on horseback who helped Genghis Khan to establish his vast empire. Archery has been a favorite among Mongolians for centuries: they regard the bow and arrow as a symbol of manhood, a weapon and also a mascot to carry everywhere. Archery competitions at the *Nadam* Fair are exciting to watch: the competitors, wearing narrow-sleeved tight robes, draw their bows while galloping on horseback and manage to shoot their arrows right on target.

Horse racing: This is the most eye-catching event at a *Nadam* Fair. Mongolians grow up on horseback and horses play a very important part in their lives. Every Mongolian loves to prove his worth by showing good horsemanship, which they practice tirelessly from a very young age.

Since the establishment of the Inner Mongolia Autonomous Region, the *Nadam* Fair has become a major gathering of Mongolian people with modern characteristics. At the fair, thousands of people from all over Inner Mongolia and other Mongolian settlements gather together on the

Oboo Ritual.

vast green fair site decorated with colorful flags. They wear their holiday best, drink *koumiss* (fermented mare's milk), sing folk songs, eat roast mutton, play traditional instruments and dance from dusk till dawn, celebrating with customary Mongolian enthusiasm. The *Nadam* Fair has become a joyful occasion to celebrate the harvest, national unity and Mongolian achievements. It is not only a cultural and athletic meeting with traditional games, but also includes information exchange, trade and other activities.

Fast-Breaking Festival

Name: Fast-Breaking Festival
Date: the first day of the tenth month of the Islamic calendar

The Festival of Fast-Breaking is one of the three major Islamic festivals and is celebrated by the Hui, Uygur, Kazak, Ozbek, Tajik, Tartar, Kirgiz, Salar, Dongxiang and Bonan people. Every ninth month according to the Islamic calendar is called Ramadan, which lasts for twenty-nine or thirty days. In 2009 the Fast-Breaking Festival fell on September 21, and was approximately ten days behind the Gregorian calendar. During this period, Muslims must finish their pre-fasting meal before sunrise and are not allowed to eat or drink anything until the sun goes down. In addition, all Muslim people are supposed to curb all their personal desires and practice abstinence during this time in order to show their allegiance to Allah. Children,

Hui Muslims go to the mosque for prayers.

invalids, elderly people and menstruating women are allowed not to fast but they should limit their diet and must not eat or drink in public. In the evening when the bells in the mosques ring, people can stop fasting and have a meal.

Frying sanzi.

The beginning and the end of the fasting month of Ramadan are set strictly according to when the crescent moon appears. When the month of Ramadan ends, Muslims celebrate the Fast-Breaking Festival on the first day of the tenth month of the Islamic calendar.

According to the Koran, in the early days of Islam, Muhammad, the Messenger of Allah, would mark the end of the fasting month of Ramadan by taking a bath, putting on clean clothes, walking to the outskirts of the city together with his Muslim followers, and handing out fast-breaking donations by way of atonement. This practice gradually evolved into one of the three major Islamic festivals celebrated by all Muslims throughout the world.

On the morning of the festival, adult Muslims take baths and change into their festival best before going to the mosque for prayers. Then they begin visiting relatives and friends, exchange greetings with each other, and hand out deep-fried dough twists, fried doughnuts, almonds, tea and fruit in celebration. It is also common practice for Muslims to whitewash their houses, clean their yards and have a haircut before the festival.

Korban Festival

Name: Korban Festival
Date: the tenth day of the twelfth month of the Islamic calendar

The Korban Festival in China, an annual traditional Islamic festival, falls on the tenth day of the twelfth month of the Islamic calendar and is celebrated by Chinese nationalities of the Islamic faith, including Hui, Uygur, Kazak, Ozbek, Tajik, Tartar, Kirgiz, Salar, Dongxiang and Bonan. It is called *Eid-al-Adha* in Arabic. The date for the Korban Festival is not fixed, but is usually about seventy days after the end of Ramadan.

According to Islamic tradition, once a year Muslims slaughtered a certain number of cattle and donated them to others to show their sincere faith in Allah. Ibrahim, a prophet, once promised in public that he would even slaughter his son as a sacrifice if Allah asked him to do so. In a dream, Ibrahim received Allah's message to carry out his promise by slaughtering his son as a sacrifice. The dream returned several times and finally Ibrahim painfully made up his mind. On the next day, the tenth day of the final month according to the Islamic calendar, a tearful Ibrahim took his son to a hilltop. When he was about to carry out the order, a messenger sent by Allah descended with a sheep, and asked Ibrahim to sacrifice the sheep instead of his own son. That day was said to be the tenth day of the twelfth month of the Islamic Calendar. Since then Muslims have been marking the day by slaughtering sheep. This

Butchering oxen and sheep at Korban.

gradually evolved into the *Eid-al-Adha*, one of the most important Islamic festivals.

During Korban, all Islamic families clean their houses and make various cakes for the festival. All families owning more than a certain number of animals butcher sheep, camels or cows. The sheep to be slaughtered must be more than one year old and the cows more than two years old. The families can keep one-third of the slaughtered cattle for themselves but should distribute the rest to the poorest people and relatives.

On the morning of Korban, Islamic people tidy their clothes after taking a bath and listen to the Imams' interpretation of the Koran in mosques. It is the largest gathering in mosques of the year. After prayers and rites, families go to the graveyard to pay tribute to their departed loved ones.

Korban also provides a great opportunity for socializing and many Muslims get together and share mutton, cakes, melons and other fruit.

Beating iron drums to celebrate the holiday.

In the Xinjiang Uygur Autonomous Region, Muslims are given three days' holiday to celebrate the Korban Festival. In the Ningxia Hui Autonomous Region, all civil servants, whether they are Muslim or not, are given one day's leave on Korban. Islamic associations across China also organize gatherings during the Korban Festival.

Tibetan New Year

Name: Tibetan New Year
Date: the first day of the Tibetan calendar

Most Tibetans live in the Tibet Autonomous Region but there are also Tibetan communities in Qinghai, Gansu, Sichuan and Yunnan provinces.

The Tibetans originated from an agricultural tribe living along the middle reaches of the Yarlung Zangbo River in Tibet. In the seventh century, King Songzan Gampo began to rule the whole of Tibet and made "Losha" (today's Lhasa) the capital of his kingdom, which is called "Tubo" in Chinese historical documents dating from the Tang and Song dynasties.

Sunning the Buddha on New Year's Day.

The Tibetans, with a population of 5,146,000 according to the fifth national census in 2000, have their own spoken and written language, which belongs to the Tibetan branch of the Tibeto-Burman group of the Sino-Tibetan language family.

The Tibetan language has three major local dialects according to geographical divisions. The Tibetan script, an alphabetic system of writing, was created in the early seventh century and is used to this day in all areas where Tibetans live.

The Tibetans believe in Lamaism, which belongs to the Mahayana School of Buddhism but which has assimilated some of the beliefs and rites of the local religion known as *Bon*. There are lamaseries all over Tibet and many Tibetan festivals have a strong religious flavor. Tibetans' social life and customs and habits reflect their historical traditions and distinctive culture.

The Tibetans have their own calendar, which was systematized in 1027. Written records show that the Tibetans invented their own calendar (called the *Bon* Calendar) before 100 BC. As cultural exchanges between the Tibetans and the Han people increased, the Tibetan calendar eventually became quite similar to the lunar calendar followed in areas inhabited by the Han. Under the rule of the Sagya Monastery, the Tibetan calendar was fixed as well as the ceremonies to celebrate the Tibetan New Year, and has remained unchanged since then.

The Tibetan calendar designates the years by five elements (metal, wood, water, fire and earth) and twelve animals, which represent the twelve Earthly Branches. A year is thus divided into four seasons and twelve months, which have twenty-nine or thirty days. For example, according to the Tibetan calendar 2009 is the Year of Earth Ox and 2010 the Year of Iron Tiger. Normally quite close, the Tibetan New Year in 2009 was ten days behind the Spring Festival of the Han.

The Tibetan New Year is the most important festival in Tibet. Tibetans begin preparing for New Year's Day early in the twelfth month of the Tibetan calendar. As well as preparing food, each household has to prepare a "Five-Cereal Container" which is a richly carved, brightly painted wooden box containing fried highland barley mixed with butter with flowers made of butter and green shoots of highland barley on top. This is done to pray for a bumper harvest and prosperity in the coming year.

Tibetans also put highland barley grains into a bowl of fresh water so that they can grow into green shoots of one or two inches by the New Year. They fry wheat dough mixed with butter in various shapes as religious offerings and for guests.

On the eve of the Tibetan New Year, Tibetans clean up their houses, change their door and window curtains, set up new prayer flags on the roof and paint patterns with lime on the gates, symbolizing eternity and good luck. In the evening, family members gather and a good luck dinner is served. The main dish is dough drops known as Gutu in Tibetan, which have stone, wool, hot pepper, charcoal or coins inside. These items are said to predict the fortune of the person finding them. For example, stone implies a cruel heart, wool stands for a soft heart, charcoal for a black heart, hot pepper for tough talking and coins for good luck.

The Tibetan people usually do not go out or visit each other on the first day of the Tibetan New Year. From the second day, they will dress in their holiday best and greet each other with the lucky words *tashi delek*, and present ceremonial scarves called *khadas* to each other. There is singing and dancing, as well as traditional Tibetan opera, in the towns and villages across Tibet during this period. On the fifteenth day, religious activities take place in most Tibetan areas.

Tibetan women with prayer wheels.

Shoton Festival

Name: Tibetan *Shoton* Festival
Date: August (the first day of the seventh month of the Tibetan calendar)

The *Shoton* Festival, also known as the Tibetan Opera Festival, is one of the grandest traditional festivals in Tibet. In the Tibetan language, "*Sho*" means yogurt, or sour milk, and "*Ton*" means banquet. However, with the passage of time, the *Shoton* Festival has become a festival of traditional Tibetan opera. It is celebrated mainly in Lhasa and Xigaze.

The festival was a purely religious event prior to the seventeenth century. The founder of the *Gelugpa* (Yellow Sect of Buddhism), Tsongkhapa, ruled that lamas must remain in monasteries between the fifteenth and thirtieth day of the sixth month of the Tibetan calendar so as to avoid treading on and killing small creatures. The ban is lifted on the first day of the seventh month according to the Tibetan calendar. On this day all lamas can go out, accept yogurt served by local people and then enjoy the entertainment of folk songs and dances. This is said to be the origin of the *Shoton* Festival.

In early times, Drepung Monastery was the center of the *Shoton* Festival and it was known as the Drepung *Shoton* Festival. In the middle of the seventeenth century, the fifth Dalai Lama moved his residence from Drepung Monastery to the Potala Palace and added opera performance to this festival. At that time, Tibetan operas were first performed at Drepung Monastery on the thirtieth of the

Tibetan opera performance.

Tibetan opera performance.

sixth month of the Tibetan calendar and moved to the Potala Palace to be performed for the Dalai Lama on the next day.

However, after Lhasa's Norbulingka was built in the early eighteenth century as the summer residence of the Dalai Lama, it soon became the main venue of the *Shoton* Festival. Lay people have since been permitted to visit Norbulingka during the festival days.

During the festival, there are stage performances and other recreational activities in Norbulingka over several days, making for a very lively atmosphere. Tibetan opera troupes or folk dance groups from Tibet, Qinghai, Gansu, Sichuan and Yunnan all come to perform. Tens of thousands of people, carrying colorful cloth bundles and buckets of highland barley wine, arrive in Norbulingka. On carpets beneath the trees or beside multi-colored tents, with wine, food and desserts outside, they chat, drink, sing and dance all day.

In recent years the *Shoton* Festival has expanded to include major cultural events, academic seminars and trade opportunities.

Bathing Festival

Name: Tibetan Bathing Festival
Date: from the sixth to the twelfth of the seventh month of the Tibetan calendar

The Tibetan Bathing Festival is one of traditional festivals in Tibet. Since it lasts seven days, it is also known as Bathing Week.

The seventh month of the Tibetan calendar is thought to be the best time for bathing in Tibet. The rainy season has just ended and a gentle sun shines. The temperature beside the rivers is more than twenty degrees centigrade at this time.

When the sacred planet Venus appears for one week in the southern sky, all the people in Tibet go to the banks of Lhasa River, Yarlung Zangbo River and other rivers for bathing. They take carts or go on horseback, bring butter tea, wine and food, set up tents or big umbrellas along rivers and then enjoy bathing all day.

Usually, Tibetans start the day with washing their quilts, clothes and shoes in the river. At noon, when the river water has warmed up, they jump into the river. Male and female, young and old, swim, play games and bathe all together. In the afternoon, most people have a party in their tents or under trees, where they drink, sing, dance and have fun until Venus reappears in the sky. They then pack up and go home.

The Bathing Festival goes back at least seven or eight hundred years in Tibet and there are many legends about its origin. One of the stories goes that there was a great doctor living in Tibet, called the Medicine King on account of his magical skills. When he died, he became a god in heaven. One year, a terrible disease struck the whole of Tibet, killing many people and cattle. The Tibetans turned to the Medicine King, and prayed for his help. When the Medicine King heard their prayers, he turned himself into a bright star. When the star shone over the hills, all the plants on the hills became medicinal and when the star shone over the rivers, the river water turned into liquid medicine.

During this night, everyone in Tibet had the same dream: a new bright star rose in the sky over southeastern Lhasa and a slim, dark girl went into the clear Lhasa River to bathe in the starlight. When she got out of the water, she was healthy and beautiful. People believed that the dream was created by the magic of the Medicine King himself and the Tibetans then all went into the river to bathe. After seven days, the new star disappeared, and so did the sickness: all had recovered. Since then, Tibetans have bathed in the river during this seven-day period and it later developed into a festival.

Tibetan astronomical documents say that at the time between the end of summer and the beginning of autumn, the rivers are cool, soft, light, clear and smell fresh. Drinking it will harm neither the throat nor the stomach. Therefore, the Bathing Festival is said to be the best time to bathe in the rivers of Tibet.

Tibetan boys bathing in the Yarlung-zangbo River.

Torch Festival

Name: Torch Festival
Date: the twenty-fourth of the sixth lunar month

With a population of 7,762,300 according to the 2000 national census, the Yi ethnic group lives mainly in Yunnan, Sichuan, Guizhou and Guangxi. The Yi language belongs to the Yi branch of the Tibeto-Burman group of the Sino-Tibetan language family and has six dialects. Yi characters, the earliest syllabic script in China, were introduced in the thirteenth century and more than 1,000 of them are still commonly used today.

The Yi people used to believe in many gods and worshipped their ancestors. In Yunnan and Guizhou, many Yi people follow Buddhist and Taoist beliefs.

The Yi people have many traditional festivals, of which the Torch Festival is the grandest and the most important. It is also known as the "*Xinghui* (return of the stars) Festival." The festival has several origins according to various legends. One tells of a wrestling contest between an ancient Yi hero and a god on the twenty-fourth of the sixth lunar month. They were both very strong but in the end the Yi hero killed the god, leaving another god very angry. In revenge, the god sent huge swarms of locusts to the earth that ate almost all the crops in three days and three nights. The Yi people had to use torches to drive the locusts away and three days and three nights of burning got rid of all the locusts. From this time on, Yi people light torches on that day with the intention of killing harmful insects and ensuring a bumper harvest.

Yi people start preparing for the Torch Festival one month in advance. Children go to hills and open fields gathering dry, long, straight pieces of wormwood for making torches. In the Liang Mountain area, Yi people usually only use wormwood, instead

of bamboo shoots or pine branches, to make torches since they believe wormwood can help against evil. The number of torches prepared depends on the number of people in the family. They will prepare at least three torches for each person, and everyone wishes to have many torches and for them to be as long as possible.

At the same time, parents prepare food for the sacrificial rites and holiday clothes for every family member. Girls need to have colorful turbans and skirts ready and even make Yi-style suits, waistbands or embroidered wallets for their lovers. Young men also buy silver earrings, blue capes or yellow umbrellas for girls with whom they are in love. Every household buys a large amount of festive food including wine, sweets, noodles and fruit, while the whole village will get together to buy one or more cows and kill them during the festival as sacrifices for the Fire God.

Finally, the twenty-fourth day of the sixth lunar month arrives. The Yi people first clean their houses in the morning. Then everyone dresses in their holiday best. Women

Young Yi people singing and dancing.

The night of the Torch Festival.

are busy cooking; men are busy killing cows and distributing the meat. The Yi people believe that eating beef on that day will bring them good luck and a peaceful life throughout the coming year.

When night falls, the Yi people will have a grand family dinner and worship their ancestors and gods. Then the torch parade begins. Men and women of all ages hold up their torches, shout lucky words and walk around their houses and fields. The torches burn like flying fire dragons in the hills, lighting up the fields and villages and banishing evil.

Then the villagers, in their holiday best, will gather at the main festival site and put their torches together to make a big bonfire. The bonfire party usually lasts till the next morning, with young Yi men blowing flutes, plucking moon-shaped instruments and three-stringed guitars while dancing, young women dancing to the rhythm and clapping their hands. Bright flames leap up to the sky, crackling and shouts of joy mingle together with the sound of the gongs and drums.

In the daytime, the Yi people watch wrestling, horse-racing, bullfights and other spectacles. The festival now combines the traditional ceremony with tourism and trade.

Many other ethnic groups including Bai, Naxi, Hani, Lahu and Pumi also celebrate the Torch Festival.

Pan Wang Festival

Name: *Pan Wang* (King Pan) Festival for the Yao people
Date: the sixteenth day of the tenth lunar month

The Yao people, with a population of 2,637,400 according to the national census in 2000, live mainly in the mountain areas in the Guangxi Zhuang Autonomous Region, as well as in Hunan, Yunnan, Guangdong and Guizhou provinces. The Yao people have their own spoken language, though many Yaos are also familiar with the Han and Zhuang languages. Yao does not appear in a written form, so Chinese is used in writing.

King Pan (*Pan Wang*) is regarded as the founder of the Yao ethnic group. For this reason, the Yao people celebrate this grand traditional festival to pay tribute to their ancestors. They also hold a big singing event during the festival.

According to legend, in a very ancient time, there was a war between King Ping of the Yao Mountain and King Gao. In order to win the war, King Ping offered his most beautiful daughter, the third princess, in marriage to whoever could bring back King Gao's head.

Unexpectedly, on the following day, a dragon-dog appeared to see King Ping with the head of King Gao in its mouth. King Ping kept his promise so the dragon-dog married the princess. However, the dragon-dog, called Pan Hu, wanted to become human. He asked the princess to steam him for seven days and seven nights. After six days and six nights of steaming, fearing that her husband was steamed to death, the princess opened the steam box, and her husband had turned into a well-built man. After that, Pan Hu was sent by his father-in-law to rule the Kuaiji Mountain as King Pan. Years passed and the couple had six sons and six daughters, who later became the founders of the twelve clans of Yao.

One day, while hunting in the mountains, Pan was pushed off a cliff by an antelope and died. The children caught the antelope and made a drum out of the antelope's hide, which they beat hard to express their anger and sorrow at their loss. This legend is believed to be the origin of the *Pan Wang* Festival. Since Pan was originally a dragon-dog, to this day eating dog is a taboo for the Yao people.

Today, *Pan Wang* Festival has gradually evolved into a happy holiday for the Yao to celebrate a good harvest and worship their ancestors. Young Yao people sing love songs to choose a sweetheart or to express their love for each other.

Yao troops on parade with a huge portrait of King Pan.

Danu Festival

Name: *Danu* Festival for Yao people
Date: the twenty-ninth of the fifth lunar month

The *Danu* Festival, also known as the Ancestral Mother Festival or the Yao New Year, is one of the grandest traditional festivals of the Yao ethnic group. It takes place on the twenty-ninth of the fifth

lunar month. This festival is only celebrated every two, three or even five years and in some Yao communities, the *Danu* Festival is only celebrated every twelve or thirteen years.

There is a famous legend about the origin of this festival. In very ancient times, there were two great magic mountains facing each other. The left one, looking like a great warrior, was called Buluosi. In contrast, the right one, looking graceful like a young girl in dress, was called Miluotuo. Every year they got a little bit closer together. After 995 years, the two mountains were actually getting near to each other. On the twenty-ninth of the fifth lunar month of this year, a deafening thunderbolt suddenly struck the earth and at exactly the same time, the two mountains cracked. A man called Buluosi came out of the mountain called Buluosi, while a woman called Miluotuo came out of the mountain of that name. They married and had three daughters. When Miluotuo grew old, she said to her three daughters: "Children, now that you have grown up, you must live on your own." So her eldest daughter, carrying ploughs and harrows, settled on the plains and lived by growing crops. Her offspring are the Han people. The second daughter left with a pile of books and her children founded the Zhuang people. The youngest daughter, taking millet and hoes, developed paddy fields and planted different kinds of crops on the mountainsides. She became the founder of the Yao people. Soon afterwards, the youngest daughter came back to her mother's home in tears, telling Miluotuo that her crops had been eaten by field mice, other animals and birds. To try to help her, Miluotuo gave her a copper drum and a cat. In the following year, the beasts and birds came back to the third daughter's fields. But this time, following her mother's advice, the daughter beat the copper drum and scared them away. Meanwhile, the cat caught all the field mice. A good harvest was thus ensured in that year.

Since then, on the twenty-ninth dayof the fifth lunar month, the birthday of Miluotuo, the three daughters carried lavish gifts and came back home to join their mother and celebrate the harvest. This finally evolved into a festival celebrated by the Yao people. *Danu* means "do not forget."

Yao men beating copper drums.

Before the *Danu* festival, all the Yao families will clean their houses, prepare sticky rice cakes and rice wine and slaughter pigs and lambs in order to entertain their relatives and friends with lavish food. On the festival day, they will gather at the village common ground, singing, dancing, beating copper drums, blowing the *suona* horn (a woodwind instrument), performing martial arts and playing ball games.

Among all the festive activities, the copper drum dance, usually involving two men and a woman, is always the main attraction. The bold, flamboyant dancing accompanies the rhythmic, sonorous tunes of the copper drums. The best drum player will be given the title of King of Drum-beating and congratulated by everyone there.

After the copper drum dance, the Yao people set off dozens or even hundreds of powerful firecrackers all at the same time in the village. The person who lights the most firecrackers will be hailed as a hero.

Some Zhuang ethnic communities in the Guangxi Zhuang Autonomous Region also celebrate the *Danu* Festival.

Miao Dragon Boat Festival

Name: Dragon Boat Festival for the Miao people
Date: between the twenty-fourth and the twenty-seventh of the fifth lunar month

The Miao ethnic group has a population of 8,940,100 according to the national census carried out in 2000. They are found in Guizhou, Hunan, Yunnan, Sichuan, Guangxi, Hubei and Hainan provinces.

The Miao people have their own language belonging to the Miao-Yao group of the Sino-Tibetan language family. Traditionally, they believe in many gods and worship their ancestors and the power of nature. According to their beliefs, gods or evil spirits possess irresistible power and the blessings of gods and ancestors are needed for good fortune, having children, expelling evil spirits and getting rid of diseases.

The Han people celebrate the Dragon Boat Festival on the fifth day of the fifth lunar month every year to honor the memory of the patriotic poet Qu Yuan. However, the Miao Dragon Boat Festival, held later in the same month, has its own origin.

It is said that, once upon a time, there lived a big black dragon in the Doushui River. The dragon was very cruel to people living along the river. At the time, an old fisherman lived with his only son along the river. One day in the fifth lunar month, the dragon kidnapped the son who was fishing on the river at the time. Hearing the news, the old fisherman, in great anger and sorrow, made up his mind to kill the dragon and save his son. Carrying a steel knife and kindling, the old man dived into the dragon cave deep under the sea. He fought the dragon for nine days and nine nights and finally chopped the dragon into three pieces, saved his son from the dragon's cave and set fire to it.

Dragon Boats of the Miao people.

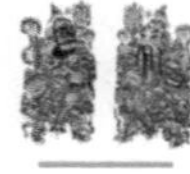

Suddenly, a pall of thick smoke hung over the Doushui River above the dragon's body as it drifted downwards. Heaven and earth were in a state of chaos and darkness. Fortunately, at that moment, a Miao girl came out to the riverbank to fetch water. She happened to drop her wooden ladle into the river. The girl immediately used her shoulder pole to get the ladle back. When the shoulder pole reached the ladle in the water, with a splash, the heaven suddenly became bright again. The darkness disappeared and the earth was bathed in sunlight once more.

To commemorate the heroic deeds of the old fisherman and the girl, the Miao people hold celebrations from the twenty-fourth to the twenty-seventh of the fifth lunar month by organizing dragon boat rowing contests along the Doushui River.

In contrast to the dragon boat used by the Han people, which is just one long, large boat, the Miao people's boat is

Splendidly dressed Miao men rowing.

made up of three canoes tied together – one large one in the middle and two small ones on the sides, made of pine. The middle one is called mother boat or main boat, while the other two are known as son boats or attached boats. The bow of the middle boat is decorated with a carved dragonhead more than one meter high and of exquisite design and craftsmanship, made from the trunk of a weeping willow and brightly painted. On the day of the contest, every dragon boat is freshly painted and decorated with colorful flags. In each boat, the coxswain rides straddling the dragon's neck on the bow of the mother boat, and beats a drum to set the pace for the oarsmen behind him. The oarsmen all wear horsetail-shaped hats, blue jackets and trousers, and embroidered waistbands pinned with silver ornaments giving them a powerful appearance.

At the start of the race the coxswain beats the drum to stir on the oarsmen, who row as hard as they can while singing folk songs. For the spectators on the riverbank, it looks like dozens of real dragons are riding the waves and advancing fast along the river.

To this day, some unique customs are still kept when the Miao people celebrate the Dragon Boat Festival. For example, villagers are allowed to send their boats down the river after the sixteenth day of the festival month, provided that they have finished weeding their fields. The sooner the boats appear on the river, the more efficient the people look. Hard-working farmers consider it shameful not to have finished weeding before the festival begins.

No matter how the oarsmen get on in their daily life, they shake hands once on board and work together as one during the race. At the end of the race, the organizers put a big duck into the river, which is then chased by all the oarsmen arriving at the finish.

Every Miao family attaches great importance to the Dragon Boat Festival and takes great care of their dragon boats. In every Miao village there is a special wooden-framed shelter with a tiled roof to house dragon boats, and because they are well cared-for, Miao dragon boats can survive dozens, or even more than one hundred, years.

Flowery Mountains Festival

Name: Flowery Mountains Festival of the Miao people
Date: between the second and seventh day of the first lunar month

The Miao people living in Yunnan and elsewhere celebrate the Flowery Mountains festival, also known as the Festival of Treading the Flowery Mountains. During this annual festival, thousands of Miao people will go to the open hillsides near their villages and hold various festive activities.

The so-called "Flowery Pole" is always the center of the festival. Usually, it is made from a long, straight length of pine or cypress. Colorful flags and prizes for pole climbing such as sweets and *lusheng* (a reed wind instrument) are hung about one meter below the top of the pole. The person who volunteers to set up the flowery pole before the first dawn of the festival will be widely acknowledged as public-spirited. The same person has the task of toasting the spectators and officially declaring the beginning of the festival, which is followed by the beating of drums and gongs and lighting firecrackers.

The festive site, full of flowers and colorful flags, becomes a sea of singing and dancing. Folk singing, *lusheng* dancing, lion dancing and bull fighting follow one another. The winner of the pole-climbing competition and the lion dance both receive a pig's head.

Lusheng dancing of the Miao people.

The festival offers a wonderful opportunity for young Miao people to find a sweetheart. Having fallen in love, the young man will present his lover with floral embroidered puttees and waistbands, while girls give out scarves and turbans they have embroidered themselves.

The Miao people in northeastern and southern Yunnan celebrate this festival on the sixth day of the sixth lunar month. Legend has it that, in ancient times, the Miao people were distressed about their ancestors' suffering. Once, on this date, their ancestors appeared and told them not to be distressed, and to cheer up, dance and play *lusheng*. After that, a flower suddenly dropped from heaven onto a tree on a hilltop. Everyone danced around the tree, playing *lusheng* and singing songs. That year there was a bumper harvest. Since then, the festival has been celebrated on that date every year.

Water-Splashing Festival

Name: Water-Splashing Festival of the Dai people
Date: between the sixth day of the sixth Dai month and the seventh day of the seventh Dai month (around mid-April in the Gregorian calendar)

The majority of the Dai people live in the Xishuangbanna Dai Autonomous Prefecture in southernmost Yunnan Province. According to the national census in 2000, the Dai population totaled 1,160,000.

The religion of the Dai is Theravada Buddhism. They also practice animistic worship by offering sacrifices to spirits and ancestors.

At the age of seven or eight, many Dai boys become a *keyong* (a novice) and are sent to the village monastery to learn the Buddhist doctrines before they join the community as a *panan* (child monk). Most Dai return to secular life around the age of seventeen or eighteen and then get married.

Splashing blessings.

Young Dai girls celebrate the Water-splashing Festival.

Former Premier Zhou Enlai celebrated the Water-splashing Festival with the Dai people in Xishuangbanna.

There are at least five dialects of Dai in Yunnan. The more popular scripts later formed the basis of the current Xishuangbanna and Dehong Dai writing. After 1949 the Chinese developed a new simplified Dai script for use among the Dai people.

The Water-splashing Festival, the New Year of the Dai calendar, held in the last ten days of the sixth month or early in the seventh month of the Dai calendar (April), usually lasts between three and five days.

Regarding the origin of the festival, legend has it that once upon a time there was a "demon of fire" who brought pain and suffering to the local people. He even forced seven women, one after another, to marry him. However, the seven women he married were brave enough to kill him. One day, the youngest and most daring of the seven women strangled the devil with his own long hair. The head of the devil fell to the ground and started rolling around. Wherever the burning head rolled was set on fire.

In order to put out the fire, the seven women in turn held the devil's blazing head in their arms, and they performed this task, each for a year. At the time of the New Year when they changed over, local people would gather to splash water on the exhausted woman to wash off the blood and dirt and refresh her. Today, the Dai people splash water at each other to commemorate the courageous act of these women who brought peace and happiness to them.

The first day of the festival is New Year's Eve. On this day, the Dai people hold the "climbing high" competition and dragon boat races. "Climbing high" refers to home-made "rockets"—bamboo canes with gunpowder in them – which are fired into the sky, leaving a curl of smoke.

The second day is a rest day as it is a day belonging neither to the old year nor the new. People usually stay at home or go hunting in the mountains.

The third day is "the king of days." In the morning, people put on their best clothes and go to temples to pray for good luck, prosperity and more children in the New Year. In the afternoon, women will wash the statues of the Buddha with water. Shortly after that, water splashing really begins.

There is a "gentle way" and a "rough way" of water splashing. The gentle way is to dip flower stems in water and sprinkle each other in blessing. The rough way involves people using bowls and buckets to soak each other. The more you are soaked, the happier and luckier you will be in the New Year.

The festival comes to a climax later in the day as the Dai people begin singing, dancing and drinking late into the night.

Besides the traditional games such as "climbing high" and dragon boat races, there is cockfighting, balloons, amusements and trading.

Third Month Street Fair

Name: Third Month Street Fair of the Bai people
Date: the fifteenth to the twenty-first of the third lunar month

The Bai are an ethnic group with a long history and unique culture who live in the Bai Autonomous Prefecture of Dali, Yunnan Province. The population numbered 1,860,000 according to the national census in 2000. The Bai have their own language, which belongs to Tibeto-Burman, a language group of the Sino-Tibetan language family.

The Street Fair is the grandest show of the year for the Bai. Held from the fifteenth to the twenty-first day of the third lunar month every year at the foot of Mount Diancang Shan, west of the ancient city of Dali, the purpose of this festival is mainly to pray for a good harvest.

The Third Month Street is also called the Market of *Guanyin*, literally meaning the Goddess of Mercy. Legend has it that in the period of the Nanzhao State (938–1253), the Goddess of Mercy came to Dali to speak about Buddhism on the fifteenth of the third lunar month, and then the Third Month Street became a temple fair for loyal believers to pay homage. Over time, and because of Dali's strategic location, the city became a prosperous trade center in the region and the market became a grand festival for the local people.

A Bai woman selling wax-printed handicrafts on the Third Month Street.

Another legend is about a "market on the moon." It is said that the third princess of Dali fell in love with a young fisherman. On the fifteenth of the third lunar month, the two went to the moon to buy fishing nets and other equipment but returned home empty-handed. The local people somehow managed to relocate the market to the earth where it began in Dali. The Bai still call the Third Month Street "Moon Street."

The traditional commodities traded at the fair are horses, mules, tea, medicine and so on. But today the site and the goods on sale are very different. As well as the market, there is horse racing, opera performances, folk singing and dancing, attracting tens of thousands of visitors, including those from other Chinese ethnic groups as well as tourists from many countries.

Moreover, the Third Month Street Fair is also an occasion for romance. In Dali, there is a famous place for people in love to visit: the Butterfly Lake. A story goes that a young couple, after undergoing many hardships, jumped into the

Still from the film *Five Golden Flowers*.

The Third Month Street.

lake to keep their love alive and were changed into butterflies. In the 1950s, a movie based on the story, *Five Golden Flowers*, was very popular across China. Today, many Chinese people still talk about the movie and can sing the theme from the soundtrack.

Double Third Singing Carnival

Name: Double Third Singing Carnival for the Zhuang people
Date: the third day of the third lunar month

Zhuang is China's largest minority group, with a population of about 16.2 million according to the national census in 2000. The majority live in the Guangxi Zhuang Autonomous Region and Yunnan province, and the rest are scattered in Guangdong, Hunan, Guizhou and Sichuan provinces. The Zhuang language is a branch of the Sino-Tibetan language family. In 1955, China developed and popularized a Zhuang writing system based on the Roman alphabet.

The Singing Carnival on the third of the third lunar month is the traditional festival for the Zhuang nationality as they excel at singing. The area where they live is known as the "Sea of Songs" or the "land carpeted with piano keys." The Zhuang, women and men alike, all begin to learn to sing at the age of four or five. They sing about love, play, work, sadness, happiness, in celebration and in mourning. They sing to urge guests to drink at parties and to urge the gods to send rain for the crops. The Zhuang even challenge each other's wit with call and response songs. The best known singers in the Zhuang's history, such as Liu Sanjie and Huang Sandi, are referred to as the "Queen of Singers" and the "King of Singers."

Now and again, the Zhuang people gather to sing songs at the Singing Carnival, usually on the third day of the third lunar month.

Liu Sanjie, the "Queen of singers" in Zhuang legend.

There would appear to be 640 meeting sites for the Zhuang in Guangxi. The Zhuang also meet at Spring Festival, Mid-Autumn or one month after the birth of a child. An impromptu singing meeting might even be staged on the way to the market.

There are songs sung on different occasions. For the "daytime singing meet," young people will gather outdoors in the fields and sing in a bid to find a partner. At the "night singing meet," the songs are usually about work, life or historical events. The songs sung at different occasions should never be confused, especially those for weddings, worship or funerals.

On the third of the third lunar month, the Zhuang from an area of up to hundreds of *li* (two *li* equal one kilometer) all dress up to meet and sing. Usually, the boys will face the girls and the girls will test the boys' character and talent through singing. Men bring gifts to the women they desire, and women throw embroidered balls tied with gifts back to the men they love.

At some singing meets, people bring colored eggs. With an egg in his hand, a young man will try to touch the egg in the hand of the woman he has a crush on. The woman, if she likes the man, will let the man to knock on her egg. If not, she will hold the egg tight, meaning that the man has no chance.

Liu Sanjie

Liu Sanjie appears as a fairy singer in a legend of the Zhuang people. It was said that she was a country girl of Zhuang nationality in the Tang Dynasty. She was born in 703, showed intelligence at an early age, and could make polished impromptu speeches when she was only twelve, making her famous in the Zhuang Region. Her songs were widely known. There are various accounts of her death. One story goes that she ran away with her lover to escape a marriage, another claims that she was killed by people envious of her brilliant talents.

Singing folk songs.

Sometimes, singing competitions will be held between villages. For instance, Village A will send a silk ball to Village B and challenge it to a folk song competition. According to the rules, Village B can only return the ball when it wins the game. If Village B loses in the competition, the embroidered silk ball will stay there. Competitions will continue in the following years until Village B wins.

Longduan Street Festival

Name: *Longduan* Street Festival for the Zhuang people
Date: in the third lunar month

Longduan Street is a grand festival popular among the Zhuang in Guangnan and Funing areas in Yunnan Province. Held in the third lunar month, the fair attracts tens of thousands of visitors every year.

The "street" here actually refers to a field dam, and the festival calls on the people to gather in the fields. The festival lasts for three to five days, during which young people will look for a partner. There will also be singing, dancing and trading.

During the festival, the Zhuang will put on the traditional Zhuang opera in a temporary open theater. With the noise of firecrackers and the beat of gongs and drums, the opera attracts crowds of visitors.

Young people are the most vibrant group during the festival. They get to know each other through dancing and singing together and even vote for "the man of the year" and "the woman of the year," judging their appearance and talents.

When a young man likes a woman, he will ask a question in song, and if the woman likes him, she will reply. The singing conversation will continue through the whole night until dawn. Men will give jewelry, cosmetics or even money to the women they like, and women will give food and fabric shoes in return. The festival is a great opportunity for the Zhuang to express their feelings of love and look for their life partner.

During the festival, the villages are all packed with visitors. It is a great opportunity for trade, with everyday goods and local produce for sale.

Zhuang opera.

Knife-Pole Festival

Name: Knife-Pole Festival for the Lisu people
Time: the eighth day of the second lunar month

The Lisu, with a population of about 634,900, live mainly in concentrated communities in the Nujiang Lisu Autonomous Prefecture in Yunnan Province. There are also small groups scattered in Sichuan Province.

According to historical records, the ancestors of the Lisu once lived along the banks of the Jinsha River and the Yalong River. Between the fifteenth and nineteenth century, they gradually migrated into the areas around the Nu and Lancang rivers. The Lisu have their own language which belongs to the Tibeto-Burman language group.

The Lisu people traditionally work in agriculture, and hunting also plays an important role in their life. They are well known for their hospitality and unique etiquette.

The annual Knife-Pole Festival on the eighth day of the second lunar month features a physical contest with a history stretching back to hundreds of years. It commemorates a Han hero sent by the Ming government who successfully drove away other ethnic groups who had intruded into Lisu lands. On the eighth, the hero, named Wang Ji, was killed by traitors on his way back to Beijing, then capital of the Ming Dynasty.

The Knife-Pole Festival is a festival exclusively for the Lisu ethnic group. On that day, people dress up and flock to watch various activities including "Climbing the Knife Pole" and "Diving into the Fire Sea."

The performers jump and dance over burning coals barefoot and half-naked, imitating animals. They even brush coals over their body and rub pieces of coal in their hands. The "fire wash"

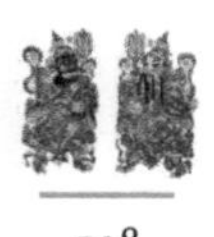

Climbing the Knife Pole.

is meant to fend off possible disasters and troubles in the New Year.

Other performers put on red clothes and red turbans. They walk up to a knife ladder which measures twenty meters long and has thirty-six sharp knives as rungs. They then kneel down in front of a picture of Wang Ji, drink a bowl of wine prepared for them and begin climbing the knife ladder. The first to reach the top will be greeted with applause and fire crackers. Amazingly, these men come down safely, with not even the slightest scratch.

This exciting and unique memorial ceremony has been officially designated as the traditional festival of the Lisu people.

New Rice Festival

Name: New Rice Festival of the Va people
Date: in the middle of the eighth lunar month

The Va people live mainly in south-western Yunnan Province with a population around 396,600. The Va people call themselves *A Va*, which literally means people who live on the mountains. Most Va people are very good at singing and dancing. In some regions, the Va people are followers of Buddhism and Christianity.

The New Rice Festival is the Va people's favorite, and autumn, when the festival is held, is their busiest time. Every morning, sounds of pounding grain can be heard on the mountains.

For the start of the festival, the Va people pick some grain that has just become ripe and bring it home. The grain is pounded into rice which is cooked and put into seven bowls, each with a large piece of meat in it. The seven bowls of rice are served with seven bowls of wine for the gods of Heaven, Earth, Mountain, Corn, and their ancestors respectively. Seven sticks of incense are also burned before an elder begins to pray. Then the new rice is sent to old people and children, who are regarded by the Va people as the purest people in the world. The

Va women pounding rice.

ritual symbolizes their worship for god and ancestors, respect for the old and love of children.

After dusk falls, the Va people gather around a fire and start to sing all night. If there is a visitor from far away, the host will offer him his best homemade wine and best chicken and rice.

The Va people are well known for their hospitality, and the etiquette with wine is worthy of note.

The host will take a drink first, brush the bamboo cup with his right hand and pass the cup with both his hands to the guest. The guest is supposed to take the wine with his right hand, with his palm uppermost, and express his gratitude. After taking a drink like the host, the guest will pass the cup to others in the same way. All people drink the wine in turn, using the same cup no matter how many guests are there.

As for the guests, they are not supposed to touch their head or ears during this process. They also should not give gifts and cigarettes to girls who might be family of the host, because this in the Va's world suggests looking for a partner.

On the second day of the festival, young men all go out to maintain the roads on which new grain will be transported into the villages. Women will be busy cleaning houses. The third day and last day of the festival also involves looking for love. After the three-day festival, the Va people formally begin their autumn harvest.

Munao Festival

Name: *Munao* Festival of the Jingpo people (*Munao* Mass Dance)
Date: the fifteenth day of the first lunar month

The Jingpo people mainly live in Yunnan Province with a population of 132,000. The Jingpo language belongs to the Sino-Tibetan language family and uses the Roman alphabet. This

Munao Festival.

ethnic group believes in a primitive religion with multiple gods. The biggest sacrifice ceremony "*Munao* Mass Dance" has turned into an annual festival, *Munao* Festival.

The "*Munao* Mass Dance" means that everyone gathers to dance. The *Munao* Festival begins on the fifteenth day of the First lunar month and lasts for four or five days. The festival mainly features singing and dancing, inviting happiness in the coming years.

The "*Munao* Mass Dance" has a long history. Legend has it that the special singing and dancing style of the Jingpo people originated from God of the Sun. It is said that only the children of the Sun can dance in that special way. Once, the birds of the Earth participated in the Sun's party and learned the dancing of *Munao*. Later, birds were dancing in the forests and the ancestors of the Jingpo people went to watch and learned the dancing from them. Surprisingly, after they had danced and sung in that way, the Jingpo people found their crops and livestock had greatly improved.

All *Munao* Festival activities are conducted around two *Munao* poles erected in the center of a big square or area of grass. The poles, made of chestnut wood, twenty meters high, and two huge shining swords placed between them symbolize the bravery and persistence of the Jingpo people. According to the Jingpo, anyone who stands on either of the two high platforms set up in front of the poles can foresee the future.

The most impressive part of the festival is the wild dancing, often involving thousands of Jingpo people.

The joyful people in their traditional clothes cheer as women wave handkerchiefs and men wave swords. The choreographed steps and sequences sometimes enact scenes of hunting, farming and daily life. The sound of traditional flutes and gongs is so loud that it seems to shake the mountains. The Jingpo people will keep dancing for up to two days.

Harvest Ceremony

Name: Harvest Ceremony for the Gaoshan People
Date: the fifth day of the eighth lunar month

The indigenous ethnic groups in Taiwan, generally called Gaoshan people in the Chinese mainland, have a population of 400,000, most of which live in the central mountain areas as well as the Zonggu Plain and Lanyu Island east of Taiwan. There are also some 4,500 Gaoshan people scattered throughout Fujian, Beijing, Shanghai and Jiangsu. They speak the Gaoshan language but write in Chinese.

The Gaoshan people traditionally practice primitive religion, believing in animism and worshipping heaven, nature and spiritual beings. Some of them converted to Christianity when it was brought to China. Their traditional festivals are all religious and basically take the form of offering sacrifices. The

Grand Harvest Ceremony.

typical ceremonies include Cultivation Ceremony, Seed-sowing Ceremony, Weeding Ceremony, Harvest Ceremony, Ancestor's Spirit Ceremony and Fishing-and-Hunting Ceremony. Among them, the Harvest Ceremony is celebrated by all Gaoshan people and is the most important.

The annual Harvest Ceremony of the Gaoshan people is equivalent to the Spring Festival of the Han people. It is held in the harvest season, usually in the eighth lunar month. Everyone, old and young, puts on their festival best: women wear flowers, brooches, earrings and bracelets; men wear feather hats (or put two or three feathers in their hair) and tie bronze bells to their waist belts. The younger people prefer small bells fastened around their ankles. People eat meat, drink wine, sing and dance, throwing themselves into the festival.

Dancing and singing is crucial for the young people to find partners. When a girl falls for a boy, she will go up to dance with him, and let her expressive steps do the talking. If a boy is adept at farming, singing and dancing, he will be popular and have more than two girls around him. The mass dance, called "Hand-in-Hand Dance," features a combination of singing and dancing without instrumental accompaniment.

The time-honored and widely popular "Hand-in-Hand Dance" has been entertaining the Gaoshan people for over a thousand years, as a daily recreation or on special occasions. Led by a talented singer, the participants sing and dance in one or more circles. The lyrics always pay homage to ancestors or legendary heroes. It is impressive to see when hundreds or even thousands of people are singing and dancing the same steps. Some men when carried away will bend down until their feather hats touch the ground before they come up again, and the excited audience will be impatient to join in.

Huijia Festival

Name: *Huijia* Festival for the Koreans
Date: varies in different areas

There are an estimated 1.92 million Chaoxian (Korean) people living in China's northeastern provinces of Heilongjiang, Jilin and Liaoning with the rest scattered in the Inner Mongolia Autonomous Region and in some cities including Beijing, Shanghai and Hangzhou. Those who live in the Yanbian Korean Autonomous Prefecture in Jilin Province speak and write Korean while those who live with the Han people simply use Chinese.

Proposing a toast to the old men.

Korean people living China usually celebrate the same festivals as the Han people, which include the Spring Festival, the Mid-Autumn Festival and the Pure Brightness Festival. The Korean people also have three famous household festivals, namely, a baby's first birthday, the *Huijia* Festival, celebrating people's sixtieth birthdays, and the *Huihun* Festival, celebrating the sixtieth wedding anniversary.

The Korean people have a long-standing tradition of respect for the aged. In their daily life, young people should never drink or smoke in front of old people or walk in front of them. If you want to pass, you should excuse yourself politely. When old people come towards you, you should step aside and give way. Young people should also use respectful language when talking to elderly people.

Huijia literally means people aged over sixty, and *Huihun* means an elderly couple who have been married for over sixty years.

Of all the ceremonial banquets held by the Koreans, the *Huijia* Banquet is the grandest. On this occasion, all relatives and neighbors will be invited for dinner to express the children's heartfelt gratitude to their parents for their birth and upbringing.

There is a story about the *Huajia* Banquet. Once upon a time, an ancient Korean king imposed a law that all people aged sixty had to be buried alive. A man named Kim, however, managed to hide his aged father to escape death. Years later, a foreign country threatened to invade Korea unless the king could answer three questions correctly. The king was desperate as he had no idea what the answers were. However, the young man went to the King and told him all the answers, and averted the crisis for the country. The king was astonished when the young man told him that the answers were given by his old father who was supposed to be buried alive. Then the king abolished the harsh law and held a grand *Huajia* Banquet to commemorate the wisdom of the elderly.

On the day of *Huijia* Festival, the Korean villages are full of happiness and fun. Every family is busy making traditional Korean food such as *tteok* cake, cold noodles and dog meat. Anyone who is sixty years old on that day will be dressed up, wear a big red flower on his chest and be seated in the middle with others sitting on both sides. His children, grandchildren and relatives will kneel down before him, taking turns to offer him wine to show their respect and gratitude.

On this day, the Koreans will dance, play on swings and wrestle, all adding to the fun of the festival.

The date of the festival varies according to different areas. In Heilongjiang Province it is held on the twentieth or twenty-fourth of the sixth lunar month, but in Yanbian Korean Autonomous Prefecture, it is held on the fifteenth of the eighth lunar month.

Filling-up-the-Storehouse Festival

Name: Filling-up-the-Storehouse Festival of the Manchu People
Date: the twenty-fifth day of the first lunar month

The Manchu, with a population of 10.7 million, are the second largest minority in China. They are mainly distributed in Liaoning Province and scattered throughout the rest of the country.

The Manchu have their own language and letters, belonging to the Manchu-Tungusic group of the Altaic language family. Manchu letters were created in the sixteenth century on the basis of Mongolian letters.

Colored models of "The marriage of the mouse girl" express wishes for a good harvest and the eradication of rodent pests. Traditional Chinese legend holds that the mouse girl married the cat, arranged as compensation to the cat for losing place his place among the twelve Chinese zodiac animals. The cat ate the mouse, thus the marriage symbolizes the eradication of mice from the home.

China's last feudal dynasty, the Qing Dynasty, was established in 1644 by the Manchu people. As Manchu people came to settle in the Central Plains from this time, the Manchus became increasingly assimilated with the Han people through frequent exchanges of trade, culture and lifestyle. The Manchu people gradually adopted the Han language.

Most Manchus traditionally believe in Shamanism, which takes the view that there are many gods commanding the world.

The Manchu and Han basically share the same festivals and holidays, such as the Spring Festival, the Lantern Festival and the Mid-Autumn Festival.

However, on the twenty-fifth of the first lunar month, Manchus celebrate the Fill-up-the-Storehouse Festival. According to the Manchu, at this time of the year, the storehouses tended to be empty. In order to fill up the storehouses, people had to go to the fields and work. On this day, every family cooks millet which will be put in a bowl and symbolically placed in the storehouse.

Meanwhile, a toy horse made of millet straw is stuck into the millet. The horse, traditional carrier of corn for the Manchu, is put there to pray for a good harvest in the coming years. Some families will instead make two hoes on this occasion. These rituals are still followed in some villages in north-eastern China.

Appendix: Chronological Table of the Chinese Dynasties

The Paleolithic Period	c.1,700,000–10,000 years ago
The Neolithic Period	c. 10,000–4,000 years ago
Xia Dynasty	2070–1600 BC
Shang Dynasty	1600–1046 BC
Western Zhou Dynasty	1046–771 BC
Spring and Autumn Period	770–476 BC
Warring States Period	475–221 BC
Qin Dynasty	221–206 BC
Western Han Dynasty	206 BC–AD 25
Eastern Han Dynasty	25–220
Three Kingdoms	220–280
Western Jin Dynasty	265–317
Eastern Jin Dynasty	317–420
Northern and Southern Dynasties	420–589
Sui Dynasty	581–618
Tang Dynasty	618–907
Five Dynasties	907–960
Northern Song Dynasty	960–1127
Southern Song Dynasty	1127–1276
Yuan Dynasty	1276–1368
Ming Dynasty	1368–1644
Qing Dynasty	1644–1911
Republic of China	1912–1949
People's Republic of China	Founded in 1949

For EU product safety concerns, contact us at Calle de José Abascal, 56–1°,
28003 Madrid, Spain or eugpsr@cambridge.org.

www.ingramcontent.com/pod-product-compliance
Ingram Content Group UK Ltd.
Pitfield, Milton Keynes, MK11 3LW, UK
UKHW020309140625
459647UK00014B/1803

* 9 7 8 0 5 2 1 1 8 6 5 9 9 *